from the kitchen of
DANIELLA SILVER

with tips & techniques from
NORENE GILLETZ

-The-

SILVER
PLATTER

simple elegance

Effortless Recipes with Sophisticated Results

Photography by **Andrea Gibson**
Food Styling & Image Consulting by **Abraham Wornovitzky**
Art Direction by **Atara Yunger**

Published by **ARTSCROLL / SHAAR PRESS**
4401 Second Avenue / Brooklyn, NY 11232 / (718) 921-9000 www.artscroll.com

Distributed in Israel by **SIFRIATI / A. GITLER**
Moshav Magshimim / Israel

Distributed in Europe by **LEHMANNS**
Unit E, Viking Business Park, Rolling Mill Road Jarrow, Tyne and Wear, NE32 3DP / England

Distributed in Australia and New Zealand by **GOLDS WORLD OF JUDAICA**
3-13 William Street / Balaclava, Melbourne 3183, Victoria / Australia

Distributed in South Africa by **KOLLEL BOOKSHOP**
Northfield Centre / 17 Northfield Avenue / Glenhazel 2192 Johannesburg, South Africa

ISBN-10: 1-4226-1834-X / ISBN-13: 978-1-4226-1834-9

Printed in Canada

Acknowledgments

To my husband **Jeffery** — what would I do without you by my side? Your love and support have fueled the passion that led me where I am today!

Emily, Alisha, and **Sorelle** — my three beautiful girlies. Your sweetness, creativity, and sense of adventure will always inspire me. This book, once again, is for you. I love watching you grow, learn, and laugh throughout the process. I love you with all my heart. XOXO

To my mom, **Resa Litwack** — you were always there behind the scenes, guiding and supporting me. You are so incredibly talented and I thank you so much for all your help!

To my sister, **Atara Yunger** — because of your brilliant design, this book embodies the simple elegance of its recipes. I am always amazed and inspired by your creativity.

To my grandparents, **Noreen and Cyril Lax** — for all your wonderful recipes to be passed down and to your excellent editing skills.

To my mother-in-law, **Bonny Silver** — thank you for inspiring me in the kitchen and for your delicious recipes.

To **Abe Wornovitzky and Andrea Gibson** — thank you for incredible photo-shoot sessions, and for making my dishes jump off the page. I still think of you both every time certain songs play on the radio. Your talent inspires me, and your friendships mean the world to me.

To my family — **Resa and Alan Litwack; Noreen and Cyril Lax; Arieh Glustein; Mena Glustein; Atara, Gadi, Neriyah, and Itai Yunger; Zvi, Naomi, Ilan, and Sari Glustein; Mike and Eden Litwack; Jonathan, Julie, Evan, and Charlotte Litwack; Bonny Silver; Hananel and Sherri Segal; Jeremy and Talya Silver** — in so many ways, this book is inspired by all of you. Family is at the heart of my cooking and creativity. I can't thank you enough for the constant love and support you have given me — both with this book and beyond.

Elise Bradt — You have done it again. Your words make me hungry! You are so articulate with the way you write and I'm so lucky to have you on my team.

Sharona Abramovitch — thank you for your help with the nutritional analyses.

To **Mary Jane Leones and Jenny Encarnacion** — thank you for being my sous chefs in the kitchen!

Gedaliah Zlotowitz — thanks for all your help and guidance throughout this journey.

To the **ArtScroll** team — **Felice Eisner, Devorah Cohen and Eli Kroen**— I am so happy to have you back on the *Silver Platter* journey for Book Two. Thanks to **Judi Dick** and **Tova Ovits** for your helpful comments and fantastic proofreading. Love working with all of you.

Norene Gilletz — to my partner in crime, Norene — I am so thankful to have had the opportunity to work with you again. I continue to be amazed by your brilliance— inside and outside the kitchen. We are all lucky to learn from your insights in Book Two!

To all my family, my friends, and the local store owners who provided me with props. Lending me all your beautiful dishes helped me so much with my photo shoots. It was honestly the biggest help you could give me and made the shoots feel seamless and fun: **Rebecca Bergel, Chayala Bistricer, Randy Brotman, Naomi Glustein, Merick Golan, Daniella Greenspan, Rivka Grossman, Aimee Hass, Emily Hershtal, Kitchen Art, Pam Kuhl, Vivian Kuhl, La Compania, Resa Litwack, Fern Orzech, Shoshana Schachter, Sherri Segal, Bonny Silver, Talya Silver, Susan Silverman, Spread INC., Chantal Ulmer, Tammy Weintraub, Dori Weiss, and Atara Yunger.**

Table of Contents

As I sit down to write this

introduction to my second cookbook, a few happy tears come to my eyes. It has been such an incredible culinary journey, creating and cooking my way through my *Silver Platter* books. So far, it's been an education, an exercise in imagination, a pursuit of passion, and, best of all, an opportunity to meet and become part of a community of amazing, creative, and talented people — especially my readers.

I have gotten such pleasure knowing how much everyone enjoyed the first *Silver Platter*, and want to thank all of you for sharing your feedback and photos. Many of you have told me that *Simple to Spectacular* has become your go-to cookbook, or that it's inspired you to return to your kitchens. It's all of you who continue to fuel my passion along this cookbook journey.

Among the most common feedback I received on my first *Silver Platter* cookbook was that the dishes were "do-able." Although I love to cook, I don't like spending hours in the kitchen. We all have very busy lives but still want to prepare healthy, fresh meals for our family and friends. When it came to writing a second cookbook, I wanted to focus on that concept even more: creating simple, elegant dishes that suit our busy schedules. I'm a busy mom, so this idea truly is the foundation of my cooking style.

Now don't let the word "elegant" scare you. For me, simple elegance doesn't mean having a list of ingredients ten pages long or using complex techniques that require charts and illustrations. My interpretation of simple elegance is turning simple ingredients into elegant dishes by paying a little extra attention to detail. It's putting that extra crunch on the top of the salad, that topping on the soup, that garnish on the chicken, or that new ingredient in the side dish. It's about putting a little inspiration in everything you do, so that even the simplest dishes become sophisticated and beautiful.

I come from a family of artists; we feel that everything beautiful comes from the details that enhance the big picture: a unique brush stroke, the angle of lighting, an extra pop of color. I have taken that knowledge and appreciation for detail and incorporated them in my recipes. I strive for every dish in my cookbook to stand out on its own, not for its complexity, but because for its attention to details and presentation. Each recipe has a color flare, a unique texture to complement an interesting form and shape; each recipe has a touch of elegance.

I hope you enjoy this cookbook as much as I have enjoyed writing it for you! And please continue sharing your thoughts and photos with me on Instagram and Facebook — you are my inspiration!

All the best, and happy eating,

XO
Daniella

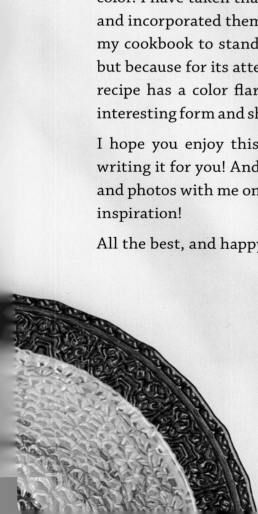

"I can't believe we get to do this again!"

That's how Norene and I launched our second culinary journey together as a team. Sitting at her kitchen table, I had just cracked open my binder of fresh new recipes, and already we were bubbling with energy to get started on "Book Two."

Norene and I are so thankful for the success of our first cookbook, *The Silver Platter: Simple to Spectacular*, which was truly a labor of love. Although we spent many months in her kitchen working together on it, we realized early on that our chemistry and special blend of talents and experiences make us a truly dynamic team.

Since the publication of our first cookbook, Norene has continued to be my culinary partner-in-crime and mentor. We've remained as close as ever — calling each other to share ideas, trading tips and tricks by email, getting together for family meals, or just enjoying a cup of tea together. When I decided that I was ready to embark on a second cookbook, I knew I had to bring Norene back on board.

We've spent countless hours in her kitchen, Norene still sipping tea and eating yogurt, me still enjoying cups of hot water and eating nuts. Between the brainstorming, the cooking, and the laughter, we've enjoyed the journey and each other's company just as much — and probably even more — as we did the first time around.

Norene and I had quickly discovered that we shared a passion for the importance of passing down family traditions from one generation of cooks to the next, as well as the need to incorporate modern twists and techniques. I'm so grateful that Norene has once again contributed her culinary wisdom to *Simple Elegance*. Ever since we first met, Norene has shared her knowledge and expertise. She has always encouraged me to try new things and tackle new challenges, and I'm so thrilled to share them with you!

For us, this book is really about encouragement. Knowing that you can do it — that you can quickly cook healthy meals that are elegant and delicious, no matter what events you have lined up on the calendar, or what guests or dietary needs you have at the table. It's been our absolute pleasure bringing this book to life, and we hope you enjoy cooking with it as much as we enjoyed creating it.

Daniella
& Norene

Appetizers

Light, refreshing, and full of color, this cooling cucumber salad is a beautiful dish to bring to the table on hot summer days. It comes together quickly and makes a great complement to grilled chicken or beef dishes.

Watermelon Radish & Cucumber Salad

pareve · passover · gluten-free · do not freeze · yields 6 servings

Ingredients

4 watermelon radishes, trimmed, halved, thinly sliced (see Norene's Notes, below)

6 baby cucumbers, thinly sliced (do not peel)

1 red bell pepper, diced

¼ cup diced red onion

¼ cup chopped fresh parsley

Dressing

¼ cup extra virgin olive oil

2 Tbsp lemon juice (preferably fresh)

2 Tbsp red wine vinegar

2 Tbsp honey

kosher salt

freshly ground black pepper

Method

1. In a large serving bowl, combine radishes, cucumbers, pepper, onion, and parsley. Cover; refrigerate.

2. **Dressing:** Combine dressing ingredients in a glass jar; seal tightly and shake well.

3. Shortly before serving, toss salad with dressing; serve.

Norene's Notes

- Watermelon radishes look like miniature watermelons. They are 3-4 inches in diameter, with a crisp red flesh and a somewhat peppery taste. The outer skin is white, with green shoulders and a pink center. They are usually available in the spring or late fall. If you can't find them, ask your local fruit market to bring them in, or substitute regular, crisp red radishes.

Bright, fragrant tomato "petals" are fanned out like flowers in this simple, elegant appetizer. Make sure the tomatoes are firm, and slice them almost to the bottom without cutting all the way through so that the "petals" open gently. Show-stopping!

Tomato Flowers
with guacamole

pareve · gluten-free · do not freeze · yields 8 servings

Ingredients

8 firm, large, ripe tomatoes, cored

Dressing

¼ cup extra virgin olive oil

¼ cup lemon juice, preferably fresh

1 Tbsp Dijon mustard

2 Tbsp pure maple syrup

2 Tbsp chopped fresh dill

Guacamole

½ cup diced red onion

1 firm, ripe avocado, peeled, pitted, and diced

Method

1. Carefully cut each tomato into 8 wedges, making sure that they are still attached at the base. Gently fan out tomato "petals" without breaking. Transfer to individual serving plates.

2. **Dressing:** Combine dressing ingredients in a glass jar; seal tightly and shake well.

3. **Guacamole:** Combine red onion and avocado in a small bowl. Drizzle with dressing. Refrigerate if not serving immediately.

4. Spoon guacamole over and into tomatoes. Serve immediately.

Norene's Notes

- Store tomatoes at room temperature until ripe. Then either use them immediately or transfer to the refrigerator.
- If you store unripe tomatoes in the refrigerator, they will be tasteless. An ideal place to ripen tomatoes is on a sunny windowsill. Sun-ripened!

Last summer, I saw that my local grocery store had beautiful fresh figs. I was inspired to create a salad that would showcase the unique flavor and texture of this succulent fruit. Simplicity at its best!

Fresh Fig & Tomato Salad

pareve · gluten-free · do not freeze · yields 6 servings

Ingredients

2 pints (4 cups) cherry tomatoes, halved

10 fresh figs, trimmed and cut into wedges

½ cup chopped fresh basil

Dressing

¼ cup extra virgin olive oil

¼ cup red wine vinegar

2 Tbsp pure maple syrup

kosher salt

freshly ground black pepper

Method

1. In a large bowl, toss together cherry tomatoes, figs, and basil. Cover; refrigerate until serving time.

2. **Dressing:** Combine dressing ingredients in a glass jar; seal tightly and shake well.

3. Gently toss salad with dressing shortly before serving.

Norene's Notes

- Variation: No fresh figs? Replace with 3-4 red pears, halved, cored, and cut into wedges (do not peel).
- Fresh figs should be ripe, sweet, and heavy. Don't rely on looks. Often, the better they look, the more tasteless they are.
- Figs are fiber-packed, full of flavor, and scattered with crunchy, edible seeds. Delicate and perishable, they are often dried, enabling us to enjoy them all year around.

This amazingly simple dish is beautiful as an appetizer and great as a side salad. A great addition to a mezze (appetizer) platter of Israeli salads and dips!

Roasted Eggplant Salad

pareve · passover · gluten-free · eggplant freezes well · yields 6 servings

Ingredients

2 medium eggplants, trimmed, diced (do not peel)

2 Tbsp olive oil

1 tsp garlic powder

1 tsp onion powder

1 tsp sweet paprika

1 tsp kosher salt

½ tsp freshly ground black pepper

¾ cup chopped fresh parsley

½ cup pine nuts (optional)

Method

1. Preheat oven to 400°F. Line a rimmed baking sheet with parchment paper.

2. In a large bowl, toss eggplant together with olive oil, garlic powder, onion powder, paprika, salt, and pepper.

3. Spread eggplant in a single layer on prepared baking sheet. Bake, uncovered, for 35-40 minutes, until golden, stirring occasionally.

4. Transfer eggplant to a serving bowl; sprinkle with parsley and pine nuts, if using. Adjust seasonings to taste. Serve at room temperature or chilled.

Norene's Notes

- How to Buy: Choose eggplants that are firm and heavy for their size, with smooth, shiny skins. Larger eggplants have tougher skins and more seeds, so small to medium eggplants are a better choice.
- To reduce eggplant's slightly bitter taste, dice it, then sprinkle with salt and let rest 30 minutes. Rinse off the salt and pat dry. This technique also extracts some of its water content, so you won't need as much oil.

It can be a real challenge finding a vegetarian dish that my husband will actually eat! Great as an appetizer, great as a main dish, or even as breakfast the next morning!

Sweet Potato Quinoa Patties

pareve · passover · gluten-free · freezes well · yields 18-20 patties

Ingredients

2 cups salted water

1 cup uncooked white or red quinoa

2 Tbsp grapeseed oil, plus more for frying

1 medium sweet potato, peeled, cut into ½-inch dice

1 medium onion, diced

2 cloves garlic, minced (about 1 tsp)

1 cup chopped baby spinach

⅓ cup panko crumbs (gluten-free or regular)

1 tsp kosher salt

freshly ground black pepper

4 eggs

Method

1. Bring salted water to a boil in a medium saucepan over high heat. Add quinoa; reduce heat. Simmer, covered, for 15 minutes or until tender. Remove from heat; let stand for 10 minutes, covered. Fluff quinoa with a fork. Let cool.

2. Meanwhile, heat oil in a large frying pan or wok. Sauté sweet potatoes, onion, and garlic for about 10 minutes, or until sweet potatoes are tender-crisp. Let cool slightly.

3. Add sweet potato mixture, spinach, panko crumbs, salt, pepper, and eggs to quinoa. Mix well. Form into patties, using a large cookie scoop.

4. Heat additional oil on medium-high heat in a large nonstick skillet. Fry patties for 2-3 minutes per side, until golden. Serve hot or at room temperature with Spicy Aioli (see Norene's Notes, below), optional.

Norene's Notes

- Variation: Instead of sweet potato, use butternut squash.
- Make sure your panko crumbs are kosher for Passover if using this recipe on the holiday.
- Spicy Aioli: In a small bowl, mix together ¼ cup mayonnaise with 2 Tbsp ketchup and 1 tsp hot sauce (or to taste). Serve with quinoa patties.

My mom has been making this simple, healthy salad since I was a kid. I like to eat this with a scoop of Easy Hummus (see Norene's Notes, below). This salad keeps well, so enjoy any leftovers throughout the week.

Colorful Chickpea Salad

pareve · gluten-free · do not freeze · yields 6-8 servings

Ingredients

2 cans (19 oz/540 ml each) chickpeas, rinsed and drained

1 red bell pepper, diced

1 orange bell pepper, diced

1 yellow bell pepper, diced

½ small red onion, diced

½ cup chopped fresh dill

Dressing

⅓ cup extra virgin olive oil

⅓ cup white vinegar

2 cloves garlic, minced (about 1 tsp)

kosher salt

freshly ground black pepper

Method

1. In a medium-sized serving bowl, combine chickpeas with peppers, onion, and dill.

2. **Dressing:** Combine dressing a glass jar; seal tightly and shake well.

3. Add dressing to salad; toss gently to combine. Adjust seasonings to taste. Cover; refrigerate. Serve chilled.

Norene's Notes

- Easy Hummus: In a food processor fitted with the "S" blade, combine ¼ cup fresh parsley, 3 cloves garlic, and 1 can (19 oz /540 ml) chickpeas, rinsed and drained. Process until minced. Add ⅓ cup oil, 3 Tbsp tahini, ⅓ cup lemon juice, 1 tsp salt, pepper, and ½ tsp cumin. Process for 2-3 minutes, until smooth and creamy, scraping down sides of bowl as needed. If too thick, add 1-2 Tbsp water. Serve chilled. Yields 2 cups.

One Shabbat morning, I decided to toss some green olives, pickles, and radishes into the beloved Israeli salad for a salty and colorful kick — what a delightful result! Brighten up your next Israeli salad with this twist on a traditional favorite.

Updated Israeli Salad

pareve · dairy option · passover · gluten-free · do not freeze · yields 6 servings

Ingredients

6 baby cucumbers, halved lengthwise and sliced into half-moons (not peeled)

1 pint (about 2 cups) cherry tomatoes, halved

4 radishes, trimmed, thinly sliced

½ medium red onion, diced

1 cup sliced green olives

5 Israeli pickles, sliced

½ cup chopped fresh parsley

Dressing

¼ cup extra virgin olive oil

¼ cup lemon juice (preferably fresh)

2 cloves garlic, minced (about 1 tsp)

1 tsp kosher salt

freshly ground black pepper

Method

1. In a medium bowl, combine cucumbers, tomatoes, radishes, onion, olives, pickles, and parsley.

2. **Dressing:** Combine dressing ingredients in a glass jar; seal tightly and shake well.

3. Shortly before serving, add dressing to salad; toss gently to combine. Cover; refrigerate. Serve chilled or at room temperature.

Norene's Notes

- Variations: Instead of green olives, use black. Add 1 jar (12 oz/340 g) artichoke hearts, diced, and 1 red bell pepper, diced.
- Dairy Variation: Sprinkle with 1 cup crumbled feta or goat cheese just before serving.

The beauty of this dish comes from its simplicity. The color combination is stunning — and the taste is spectacular. Crimson beets, creamy green avocado, fresh chives — easy, casual, elegant!

Beets & Avocado

pareve · passover · gluten-free · do not freeze · yields 4-6 servings

Ingredients

1 bunch red beets, scrubbed and trimmed (about 4 medium beets)

1 ripe avocado

3 Tbsp extra virgin olive oil

3 Tbsp lemon juice (preferably fresh)

2 Tbsp honey

kosher salt

freshly ground black pepper

¼ cup toasted slivered almonds, for garnish

chopped chives, for garnish

Method

1. Preheat oven to 350°F. Coat a large piece of heavy-duty foil with nonstick cooking spray. Center beets on foil; wrap tightly, pinching edges together.

2. Bake for 1-1½ hours, until tender. Carefully open packets; let beets stand until cool enough to handle.

3. Using a paper towel, rub off and discard skins. Slice beets into thin rounds; arrange rounds on a large serving platter.

4. Shortly before serving, peel, pit, and dice the avocado. Tuck avocado dice between beets or place them in the center of the platter.

5. Drizzle with oil, lemon juice, and honey; sprinkle with salt and pepper. Top with almonds and chives. Serve chilled or at room temperature.

Norene's Notes

- Shortcut: Buy vacuum-packed precooked beets. For even cooking when using fresh beets, choose smaller beets that are about the same size. They are fully cooked when a metal skewer glides through them easily. Beets can be cooked in advance and refrigerated.

- To prevent them from discoloring, avocados should be prepared just before serving.

Smoked salmon always adds a touch of elegance to a menu, especially for brunch. If you want to go beyond the traditional bagel option, this salad is a great alternative. With healthy fat that's full of flavor, you really can't go wrong.

Smoked Salmon Salad

pareve · passover · gluten-free · do not freeze · yields 4 servings

Ingredients

8 cups mixed greens (or 1 head romaine, torn into bite-sized pieces)

2-3 baby cucumbers, thinly sliced (do not peel)

1 cup cherry tomatoes, halved

½ cup thinly sliced red onion

8 oz/250 g good-quality sliced smoked salmon or lox

1 firm ripe avocado, peeled, pitted, diced

2 Tbsp sesame seeds

½ cup toasted slivered or sliced almonds (optional)

Dressing

⅓ cup extra virgin olive oil

⅓ cup lime juice (preferably fresh)

2 Tbsp rice vinegar

1 Tbsp soy sauce or tamari

2 Tbsp honey

1 Tbsp toasted sesame oil (optional)

pinch salt

Method

1. In a large bowl, combine salad greens, cucumbers, cherry tomatoes, and onion. Cover; refrigerate.

2. **Dressing:** Combine dressing ingredients in a glass jar; seal tightly and shake well.

3. Just before serving, drizzle dressing evenly over salad; toss to combine. Roll up salmon strips to form "roses." Add to salad along with avocado, sesame seeds, and almonds, if using. Mix gently to combine.

Norene's Notes

- Smoked Salmon or Lox — What's the Difference? Authentic lox is made from only the belly portion of the salmon, the richest and tastiest portion. It is salt-cured or brined, but never cooked or smoked. However, smoked salmon can be made from any part of the fish. It is usually covered in spices or a dry rub after curing and has more of a smoky flavor. Either one can be used in this salad — or as a topping on a crusty bagel (but not on Passover)!

Slow-cooked pulled beef brisket is an absolute must — try it with this novel nacho topping for your next party. This meaty masterpiece is worth the effort. This brisket is also delicious on its own as a main dish.

Pulled BBQ Beef Nachos

meat · gluten-free option · brisket freezes well · yields 12 servings

Ingredients

Slow-Cooked BBQ Brisket

2 large onions, chopped

1 beef brisket
(about 4 lb/2.3 kg)

kosher salt

freshly ground black pepper

2 tsp garlic powder

1 tsp chili flakes (or to taste)

2 cups ketchup

⅓ **cup** brown sugar

1 cup water or red wine

¼ **cup** vinegar

Toppings

1 bag (32 oz/900 g) tortilla chips (regular or gluten-free)

1 pint cherry tomatoes, halved

4 scallions, thinly sliced

1 avocado, peeled, pitted, and diced

sriracha or hot sauce, for drizzling

Method

1. Coat the inside of a slow cooker insert with nonstick cooking spray (see Norene's Notes, below). Add onions and brisket; sprinkle brisket on both sides with salt, pepper, garlic powder, and chili flakes.

2. Combine ketchup, brown sugar, water, and vinegar in a large measuring cup. Pour over, under, and around brisket. If you have time, marinate overnight in the refrigerator.

3. Place insert into slow cooker. Cook on low for 8-10 hours, until brisket is tender and falls apart when pulled with a fork.

4. With brisket in slow cooker, use 2 forks to pull it apart. Stir meat together with sauce. Keep warm until serving time.

5. Spread tortilla chips in a single layer on a large serving platter. Top with shredded brisket, tomatoes, scallions, and avocado. Drizzle with sriracha.

Norene's Notes

- No slow cooker? Use a large roasting pan. Cook brisket, covered, in a 325°F oven for 3-4 hours, until fork tender. Calculate 45 minutes cooking time per pound.

- Variation: Add ½ cup chopped fresh parsley and ½ cup sliced black olives along with the tomatoes, scallions, and avocado in Step 5.

This recipe couldn't get any more casual, yet it's the most popular appetizer at every party. Salty pretzels wrapped with crispy corned beef and seasoned with a spicy-sweet glaze — is your mouth watering yet?

Deli-Wrapped Pretzels

meat · gluten-free option · do not freeze · yields 8-10 servings

Ingredients

¼ cup brown sugar, firmly packed

1 tsp chili flakes (or to taste)

1 tsp cayenne pepper (or to taste)

16 long, thick pretzel rods, (regular or gluten-free) halved (see Norene's Notes, below)

1 lb/500 g sliced deli corned beef

Method

1. Preheat oven to 375°F. Line a baking sheet with aluminum foil; coat with nonstick cooking spray.

2. In a shallow medium bowl, combine brown sugar, chili flakes, and cayenne pepper. Mix well.

3. Dredge both sides of corned beef strips in seasoning mixture. Wrap 1-2 pieces of deli around the cut edge of each pretzel. Leave the rounded edge of the pretzel uncovered to use as a handle.

4. Arrange pretzels on prepared baking sheet in a single layer, with the ends of the corned beef under the pretzels so they don't unravel.

5. Bake, uncovered, for 15 minutes, until meat is golden and crisp. Serve hot or at room temperature, with dips (see Norene's Notes, below), optional.

Norene's Notes

- Cut the pretzels in half with a serrated knife or a cleaver, using firm pressure.
- Dunkin' Ideas: To serve, dip pretzels in Dijon mustard, sweet chilli sauce, or duck sauce. Yum!

These little bites of steak are simple, sophisticated hors d'oeuvres. The hoisin-based marinade tenderizes the meat, infusing each tidbit with both sweet and savory flavors. Serve these on toothpicks or on a bed of rice or quinoa as a main dish, too.

Hoisin Steak Bites

meat · freezes well · yields 6-8 servings

Ingredients

1 London broil or **3** boneless rib eye steaks (about 2 lb/1.8 kg total)

kosher salt

freshly ground black pepper

4 cloves garlic, minced (about 2 tsp)

½ cup hoisin sauce

¼ cup ketchup

3 Tbsp pure maple syrup

2 Tbsp seasoned rice vinegar

grapeseed oil, for frying

Method

1. Cut meat into ¾-inch chunks; place into a resealable plastic bag.

2. Sprinkle meat with salt, pepper, and garlic. Add hoisin sauce, ketchup, maple syrup, and vinegar. Seal tightly. Marinate for 1 hour, or up to 24 hours in the refrigerator. Turn bag over occasionally so meat is covered with marinade.

3. Remove bag from refrigerator. Remove steak from marinade; reserve marinade.

4. Heat oil in a large skillet over medium heat. Working in batches, fry meat until browned on all sides, turning meat as needed.

5. Meanwhile, pour marinade into a small saucepan; bring to a boil. Reduce heat; simmer for 5 minutes to create sauce.

6. Serve meat on small skewers or toothpicks. Drizzle sauce over meat or pour sauce into a small serving bowl for dunking.

Norene's Notes

- Variation: Instead of beef, substitute boneless skinless chicken breasts, cut into chunks.
- For a pretty presentation, spear a cherry or grape tomato on one end of each skewer.
- Leftover steak bites are a great addition to green or grain-based salads.

Heading into a nuevo world of avocado everything ... I wanted to create a pretty appetizer using avocados. This wonderful and healthy appetizer can also be served for dinner.

Stuffed Avocados

meat · gluten-free · meat freezes well · yields 8 servings

Ingredients

1 Tbsp vegetable oil

1 lb/500 g lean ground beef (or chicken, turkey, or veal)

1 pkg (1.25 oz/35 g) taco seasoning mix

4 firm, ripe avocados

juice of **1** lime (about 2 Tbsp)

1 firm, ripe tomato, diced

2 scallions, thinly sliced

½ cup roughly chopped fresh cilantro or parsley

1 Tbsp extra virgin olive oil

kosher salt

freshly ground black pepper

Method

1. Heat oil in a large skillet over medium heat. Add ground beef; cook for 8-10 minutes, until cooked through, stirring often to break up meat. Stir in taco seasoning mix; cook for 2 minutes longer.

2. Just before serving, cut avocados in half; remove pit. Scoop out about 1 tablespoon of flesh from each, dice finely, and place into a small bowl. Drizzle avocados with lime juice.

3. Spoon hot meat mixture into cavity of each avocado.

4. Add tomatoes, scallions, cilantro, oil, salt, and pepper to the diced avocados. Stir well to combine.

5. Spoon topping over stuffed avocados. Serve immediately.

Norene's Notes

- Adding the scoops of avocado to the topping mixture ensures that none of the avocado goes to waste. The diced avocado adds a tasty, creamy texture.

Soups

Hearty, colorful, and protein-packed, this Mexican-inspired soup is perfect for cold winter nights. With a dash of chili powder and a boost of lime juice, it will warm you up.

Black Bean & Tomato Soup

pareve · meat variation · gluten-free · freezes well · yields 8-10 servings

Ingredients

1-2 Tbsp olive oil

2 large onions, diced

4 cloves garlic, minced (about 2 tsp)

2 carrots, peeled and diced

2 stalks celery, diced

1 can (28 oz/796 ml) tomatoes, with their liquid

4 cups water or vegetable broth

2 cans (19 oz/540 ml each) black beans, drained and rinsed

1 tsp chili powder

1 tsp honey

2 tsp kosher salt

½ tsp black pepper

2 Tbsp lime juice (preferably fresh)

fresh chopped parsley or cilantro, for garnish

Method

1. Heat oil in a large soup pot over medium heat. Add onions and garlic; sauté for 5-7 minutes, or until golden.

2. Stir in carrots and celery. Sauté for 5-7 minutes longer, or until softened.

3. Add tomatoes with their liquid, water, black beans, chili powder, honey, salt, and pepper. Bring to a boil. Reduce heat. Simmer, partially covered, for 1 hour, stirring occasionally.

4. Remove from heat. Add lime juice; adjust seasonings to taste. Garnish with parsley or cilantro.

Norene's Notes

- Meal in a Bowl: Add 1 cup rice or quinoa, rinsed and drained, at the end of Step 3. Stir in 1 can (12 oz/340 g) corn niblets, drained. Simmer, covered, about 20 minutes longer, stirring occasionally. If too thick, add water or broth; adjust seasonings to taste.
- Meat Variation: Add 2 cups cooked chopped chicken in Step 4.
- Tomato Tip: You can use any variety of canned tomatoes in this recipe.

This delicious soup comes from my mother-in-law, Bonny Silver, who often serves it as a starter course for Yom Tov dinners. Apples, squash, brown sugar, and leeks give this soup a warm, comforting, and slightly sweet flavor for the fall season.

Squash & Leek Soup

pareve · passover · gluten-free · freezes well · yields 8 servings

Ingredients

2 Tbsp olive oil

2 leeks, trimmed, sliced (white part only)

2 cloves garlic, minced

6 cups butternut squash cubes

2 green apples, peeled, cored, chopped

¼ cup brown sugar, lightly packed

1 tsp kosher salt

¼ tsp black pepper

5 cups water or broth

Method

1. Heat oil in a large soup pot over medium heat. Add leeks and garlic; sauté for 6-8 minutes, until softened.

2. Add squash, apples, brown sugar, salt, pepper, and water. The water should just cover the vegetables. Bring to a boil.

3. Reduce heat. Simmer, partially covered, for 30-40 minutes, or until vegetables are tender, stirring occasionally. Remove from heat; let cool slightly.

4. Using an immersion blender, process soup until smooth. If soup is too thick, add a little water or broth. Adjust seasonings to taste.

Norene's Notes

• An immersion blender does a great job of puréeing soups right in the pot. When the immersion blender is immersed partway into the pot, the whirling blades create a kind of whirlpool, blending your soup to silky perfection. Cordless models are the best of the lot in terms of convenience.

Kale is still winning over kitchens everywhere. This healthy, hearty green makes a great addition to any chunky-style soup or stew because it can stand up to meat and potatoes. Here, it's a perfect partner to delicious bites of sweet potato.

Sweet Potato & Kale Soup

pareve · passover · gluten-free · do not freeze · yields 6 servings

Ingredients

1 Tbsp olive oil

1 large onion, diced

2 cloves garlic, minced (about 1 tsp)

3 large sweet potatoes, peeled, cut into large chunks

6 cups vegetable broth

2 bay leaves

1 bunch kale, trimmed, coarsely chopped

kosher salt

freshly ground black pepper

Method

1. Heat oil in a large soup pot over medium heat. Add onion and garlic; sauté for 5-7 minutes, or until golden.

2. Stir in sweet potatoes, broth, and bay leaves. Bring to a boil; reduce heat. Simmer, partially covered, stirring occasionally, for 40-45 minutes, or until sweet potatoes are tender.

3. Add kale; simmer for 10 minutes longer. Discard bay leaves. Season soup with salt and pepper.

Norene's Notes

- Variation: Instead of kale, use spinach or Swiss chard.
- There are many varieties of sweet potatoes. Skin colors can range from white to yellow to red, purple, and brown; their flesh can be white, yellow, or orange, from light to dark. Darker-fleshed sweet potatoes, which have a copper skin and orange flesh, become creamy and fluffy when cooked. These are the best choice for soups.

I love serving sweet fruit soup as a healthy alternative to cake in the hot summer months. Cinnamon adds warmth to this cold soup, while honey creates a thicker consistency. Delicious on its own as an appetizer or served with a slice of cake for dessert.

Strawberry Orange Soup

pareve · passover · gluten-free · freezes well · yields 8 servings

Ingredients

2 pints strawberries, trimmed

¾ cup orange juice

3 Tbsp honey

1 tsp ground cinnamon

¼ cup fresh basil, plus more for garnish

Method

1. Combine all ingredients in a large bowl. Using an immersion blender, purée until smooth.

2. Transfer to glass jars. Cover; refrigerate for 3-4 hours, until chilled.

3. Garnish with additional basil.

Norene's Notes

- Honey Info: Although honey never spoils, it *will* crystallize. To liquefy it, heat a saucepan of water to simmering, then remove from heat. Place the jar of honey into the water; let stand, stirring occasionally, for 10-15 minutes, until honey liquefies. You can also microwave honey briefly on medium power. If the jar has a glass lid, remove it before microwaving.

- Honey is great for most people, but it should not be given to children under the age of one year. It can cause rare but potentially fatal infant botulism.

This is a great soup to make when gardens are overflowing with zucchini. There's nothing like adding the bold flavor of fresh herbs to make a homemade soup sing. Here, the punch of dill transports you to a summer garden. A food processor helps speed up prep.

Zucchini Dill Soup

pareve · passover · gluten-free · freezes well · yields 8 servings

Ingredients

1-2 Tbsp grapeseed oil

2 large onions, chopped

2 cloves garlic, minced (about 1 tsp)

8 medium zucchini (about 2½ lb/1.2 kg), coarsely chopped

2 medium carrots, peeled, trimmed, coarsely chopped

4 cups water or vegetable broth

1 bunch fresh dill, minced (about ¾ cup)

2 tsp kosher salt

½ tsp black pepper

additional minced dill, for garnish

Method

1. Heat oil in a large soup pot over medium heat. Add onions and garlic; sauté for 5-7 minutes, or until golden.

2. Stir in zucchini and carrots. Sauté for 5-7 minutes longer, or until slightly softened.

3. Add water; bring to a boil. Reduce heat. Simmer, partially covered, for 45-50 minutes, stirring occasionally. Add dill; simmer 10 minutes longer. Cool slightly.

4. Using an immersion blender, process soup until smooth. If soup is too thick, add a little water. Add salt and pepper; adjust seasonings to taste. Garnish individual soup bowls with additional dill.

Norene's Notes

- Three medium zucchini weigh about 1 lb/500 g.
- Zucchini, also referred to as summer squash, are green, yellow, or sometimes striped. They are a high-water vegetable, so they're low in calories. They can be used in many ways, including soups, stir-fries, salads, kugels, quiches, muffins, and cakes.
- Quick Clean-Up: After chopping all the vegetables in your food processor, pour the water called for in the recipe into the emptied processor bowl and swish it around. Pour it into the soup and you'll have an almost-clean processor bowl!

Rich and rustic but light on calories, this dish has become a household favorite. The cauliflower adds that thick, creamy consistency so you can skip the cream you'd usually add to a mushroom soup.

Mushroom Cauliflower Soup

pareve · passover · gluten-free · freezes well · yields 8 servings

Ingredients

1-2 Tbsp grapeseed oil

1 large onion, diced

4 cloves garlic, minced (about 2 tsp)

6 cups button mushrooms, sliced

1 large head cauliflower, cored, cut into small florets

6 cups water or vegetable broth

2 tsp kosher salt

freshly ground black pepper

1 tsp minced fresh thyme leaves, plus additional whole thyme leaves, for garnish

Method

1. Heat oil in a large soup pot over medium heat. Add onion and garlic; sauté for 6-8 minutes, or until softened.

2. Add mushrooms; sauté for 5 minutes longer, until softened.

3. Stir in cauliflower, water, salt, pepper, and thyme; bring to a boil. Reduce heat. Simmer, partially covered, for 30-40 minutes, or until cauliflower has softened, stirring occasionally. Cool slightly.

4. Using an immersion blender, process soup until smooth. If soup is too thick, add a little water. Adjust seasonings to taste. Garnish with additional thyme leaves.

Norene's Notes

- Buying Tips: Look for thick, compact heads of cauliflower with creamy white florets.
- Storage Tips: Store unwashed cauliflower in the refrigerator in an open or perforated bag, stem-side down, for up to a week. Pre-cut florets will stay fresh for 2-3 days.
- Preparation: Don't wash cauliflower until it's ready to be used. Soak in salt water or vinegar and water to help force out any insects lodged between the florets. Remove outer leaves; then cut away the stalk with a sharp knife. Cut each cluster from the core, leaving a little bit of the stem with each cluster. Cut into florets.

This soup was inspired by my delicious, crunchy chickpea snack from my first book. I thought it would make a great textural addition to cauliflower soup, and I was right. Easy and super healthy, this soup is great for any occasion.

Roasted Cauliflower & Chickpea Soup

pareve · gluten-free · freezes well · yields 8 servings

Ingredients

1 medium head cauliflower, cored, cut into small florets

2 medium onions, cut into 1-inch chunks

1 can (19 oz/540 ml) chickpeas, rinsed and drained

2 Tbsp olive oil

4 cloves garlic, minced (about 2 tsp)

kosher salt

freshly ground black pepper

1 tsp sweet paprika

1 tsp turmeric

1 Tbsp honey

5 cups water or vegetable broth

Method

1. Preheat oven to 400°F. Line a rimmed baking sheet with parchment paper.

2. Place cauliflower, onions, and chickpeas onto prepared baking sheet. Drizzle with olive oil; sprinkle with garlic, salt, pepper, paprika, turmeric, and honey. Mix well. Spread in a single layer.

3. Bake, uncovered, for 35-40 minutes, or until cauliflower is tender-crisp. Let cool. Remove ½ cup of mixture; set aside to use as a garnish.

4. Transfer remaining mixture to a large pot. Add water; bring to a boil. Reduce heat. Simmer, uncovered, for 12-15 minutes, stirring occasionally. Remove from heat; cool slightly.

5. Using an immersion blender, process until smooth. If soup is too thick, add a little water. Adjust seasonings to taste. Serve in individual soup bowls, garnished with a spoonful of reserved chickpea-cauliflower mixture.

Norene's Notes

- For tips on buying, storing, and prepping cauliflower, see Norene's Notes on page 50.
- Cauliflower often has discolored areas or blemishes. An easy way to remove them is to use a rasp-style grater, the same kind you use to zest lemons. Clean cuisine!
- Color Your World: Cauliflower comes in a rainbow of colors. Purple cauliflower turns green when cooked. Orange cauliflower, because of its high beta-carotene content, is about 25 percent higher in vitamin A than white cauliflower.

When Rosh Hashanah rolls around, this is one of my favorite first courses. Wonderfully warming, with a sprinkling of spiced pumpkin seeds for crunch, this soup is also perfect for Succot and Thanksgiving.

Pumpkin Soup
with pumpkin crunch

pareve · gluten-free · freezes well · yields 8 servings

Ingredients

Pumpkin Crunch

1 cup shelled pumpkin seeds

1 Tbsp olive oil

1 Tbsp pure maple syrup

½ tsp ground cinnamon

Soup

1 Tbsp olive oil

1 large onion, diced

4 cloves garlic, minced (about 2 tsp)

2 cans (14 oz/398 ml each) pumpkin purée

2 medium sweet potatoes, peeled, cut into chunks

2 Tbsp pure maple syrup

1 tsp ground cinnamon

1 tsp ground ginger

2 tsp kosher salt

½ tsp black pepper

4 cups water or vegetable broth

Method

1. **Pumpkin Crunch:** Preheat oven to 350°F. Line a rimmed baking sheet with parchment paper.

2. Scatter pumpkin seeds onto prepared baking sheet. Drizzle with oil and maple syrup; sprinkle with cinnamon. Mix well; spread evenly. Bake, uncovered, for 12-15 minutes, until glazed. Allow to cool.

3. **Soup:** Heat oil in a large soup pot over medium-high heat. Add onion and garlic; sauté for 5 minutes, or until golden.

4. Add pumpkin, sweet potatoes, maple syrup, cinnamon, ginger, salt, pepper, and water; bring to a boil.

5. Reduce heat. Simmer, partially covered, for 20-25 minutes, stirring occasionally. Remove from heat; cool slightly.

6. Using an immersion blender, process soup until puréed. If soup is too thick, add a little water. Adjust seasonings to taste. Transfer to individual soup bowls; garnish with Pumpkin Crunch.

Norene's Notes

- Pumpkin Crunch is great for munching! Why not make a double (or triple) batch? It's great as a topping for salads, breakfast cereal, or even on ice cream and frozen yogurt!

- Make It Yourself: A can (14 oz/398 ml) of pumpkin purée (about 1¾ cups) is equivalent to about 2½ lb/1.3 kg fresh pumpkin. Cut pumpkin into large chunks, discarding stem, pulp, and seeds. Bake, covered, at 400°F for 1¼ hours. Discard skin. Purée until smooth.

Tomato soup brings me back to my childhood, when my mom was forever making this simple dish. I wanted to rethink her recipe using protein-rich quinoa to make tomato soup a heartier meal-in-one. Same great flavor and bright color, and ready in 30 minutes.

Tomato Quinoa Soup

pareve · passover · gluten-free · freezes well · yields 8 servings

Ingredients

1½ cups lightly salted water

⅔ cup red or white quinoa

1 Tbsp olive oil

1 large red onion, diced

2 cloves garlic, minced (about 1 tsp)

2 cans (28 oz/796 ml each) tomatoes, with their liquid

2 tsp dried oregano

1 tsp kosher salt

freshly ground black pepper

¼ cup minced fresh chives, for garnish

Method

1. Bring lightly salted water to a boil in a medium saucepan over high heat. Add quinoa; reduce heat. Simmer, covered, for 15 minutes, or until tender. Remove from heat. Let stand for 10 minutes, covered. Fluff quinoa with a fork.

2. Meanwhile, heat oil in a large soup pot over medium heat. Add onion and garlic; sauté for 5-7 minutes, or until golden.

3. Stir in tomatoes with their liquid, oregano, salt, and pepper; bring to a boil. Reduce heat. Simmer, partially covered, for 20-25 minutes, stirring occasionally. Remove from heat; cool slightly.

4. Using an immersion blender, process until smooth.

5. Transfer soup to individual bowls; top with a scoop of quinoa. Garnish with chives.

Norene's Notes

- Kitchen Hack: Chives have a tendency to roll all over your cutting board, which can make them difficult to chop or mince. Secure the bunch on one end with a rubber band to hold them together, and then mince finely with a sharp knife.
- Tomato Tip: You can use any variety of canned tomatoes in this recipe.

Naturally thick and creamy, this potato soup is a perfect cold-weather get-together soup. An easy way to enhance its elegance is to garnish each bowl with some sautéed leeks. Serve with a thick-cut slice of toasted French baguette. Bon appetit!

Cheesy Potato Leek Soup

dairy · pareve option · passover · gluten-free · freezes well · yields 8 servings

Ingredients

1-2 Tbsp grapeseed oil

1 bunch leeks, trimmed and sliced, white and light green parts only (from about 3-4 leeks)

4 cloves garlic, minced (about 2 tsp)

3 stalks celery, trimmed, sliced

6 medium potatoes, peeled, cut into chunks

6-7 cups water or vegetable broth

2 bay leaves

2 tsp kosher salt

freshly ground black pepper

1 cup grated Cheddar or Parmesan cheese, for sprinkling

scallions, thinly sliced, for sprinkling

Method

1. Heat oil in a large soup pot over medium heat. Add leeks and garlic; sauté for 6-8 minutes, or until softened.

2. Add celery, potatoes, water, bay leaves, salt, and pepper. The water should just cover the vegetables. Bring to a boil.

3. Reduce heat. Simmer, partially covered, for 35-40 minutes, or until potatoes are tender. Stir occasionally. Remove from heat; cool slightly. Discard bay leaves.

4. Using an immersion blender, process soup until smooth. If soup is too thick, add a little water. Adjust seasonings to taste. Garnish with cheese and scallions in each bowl.

Norene's Notes

- Variations: Instead of potatoes, substitute 4 large sweet potatoes. For a lower carb soup, use half broccoli or cauliflower and half potatoes.
- Pareve Option: Omit cheese. Still very delicious!
- How to Clean Leeks: Trim off most of the green part of each leek. Make 4 lengthwise cuts almost to the root so that each leek resembles a broom. Fill the sink with cold water and swish leeks back and forth to remove any sand or grit. Dry well. Cut off and discard root end.

After we devoured our second bowl of this delicious soup, my sister, Atara, refused to believe me when I explained how quick and easy it was to make. No preservatives, no sugar — this restaurant-quality pea soup is perfect for cozy winter dinners.

Thick & Hearty Split Pea Soup

pareve · gluten-free · freezes well · yields 8 servings

Ingredients

2 Tbsp olive oil

2 large onions, diced

2 carrots, thinly sliced

2 stalks celery, thinly sliced

4 cloves garlic, minced (about 2 tsp)

1 tsp turmeric

6-7 cups boiling water or vegetable broth

1½ cups dried green split peas, rinsed and drained

2 bay leaves

2 tsp kosher salt

freshly ground black pepper

¼ cup minced fresh dill

Method

1. Heat oil in a large soup pot over medium-high heat. Add onions; sauté for 5 minutes, or until golden.

2. Add carrots, celery, garlic, and turmeric. Reduce heat to low; cook until the onions have caramelized, 8-10 minutes, stirring occasionally.

3. Add water, split peas, and bay leaves; bring to a boil. Reduce heat. Simmer, partially covered, for about 2 hours, or until peas are tender. Stir occasionally. Add salt, pepper, and dill; simmer 10 minutes longer.

4. Remove and discard bay leaves. If soup is too thick, add a little water. Adjust seasonings to taste.

Norene's Notes

- Split peas are packed with protein, fiber, iron, and B vitamins. It's not necessary to soak them before cooking — a quick rinse under running water and they are ready to go. Green or yellow split peas both work well in this recipe.
- Variation: Add ½ cup pearl barley, rinsed and drained, at the beginning of Step 3. Add more liquid in Step 4 if soup becomes too thick.

Salads

This colorful mix of Asian-inspired ingredients is hearty and satisfying. This dish will keep for a few days in the refrigerator, so it's perfect for the busy hostess. Your vegetarian guests will love you for it — and so will everyone else!

Edamame & Radish Salad

pareve • gluten-free • yields 8 servings

Ingredients

1 pkg (12 oz/340 g) frozen shelled edamame beans

6 radishes, trimmed and julienned

¼ cup diced red onion

3 scallions, thinly sliced

3 Tbsp black sesame seeds

Dressing

¼ cup extra virgin olive oil

¼ cup rice wine vinegar

2 Tbsp lime juice

2 Tbsp pure maple syrup

1 Tbsp toasted sesame oil (optional)

1½ tsp kosher salt

freshly ground black pepper

Method

1. Bring a medium saucepan of salted water to a boil. Add edamame beans; boil for 3-5 minutes, until tender-crisp. Drain well. Place into a bowl of ice-cold water for a few minutes to help them retain their bright green color. Drain well; pat dry.

2. In a large bowl, combine edamame beans with radishes, onion, and scallions. Add dressing ingredients; toss well. Cover; refrigerate until serving.

3. Adjust seasonings to taste at serving time. Sprinkle with black sesame seeds just before serving.

Norene's Notes

• Sesame Allergy? Substitute lightly toasted pumpkin seeds or sunflower seeds. They will add crunch to your lunch!

• To prevent rancidity, store sesame seeds in a tightly sealed container in a cool, dry place. They can also be stored in the refrigerator or freezer.

• Sesame seeds are high in protein and rich in fiber and fat. They are also a great source of B vitamins and minerals, including magnesium, calcium, iron, and zinc.

There's something about combining a crunchy fresh vegetable with a sweet summery fruit. This salad is no exception — although it is exceptional!

Crisp Summer Salad

pareve • gluten-free • yields 8 servings

Ingredients

5 ears corn, husked and cleaned

1 lb/500 g snap peas, trimmed, cut into bite-sized pieces

2 mangoes, peeled and diced

2 scallions, trimmed and thinly sliced

½ cup chopped fresh basil

Dressing

⅓ cup olive oil

⅓ cup lime juice, preferably fresh

2 Tbsp pure maple syrup

2 tsp Dijon mustard

kosher salt

freshly ground black pepper

Method

1. Bring a large pot of lightly salted water to a boil. Add corn; simmer for 5-7 minutes, until tender-crisp. Drain corn; place into ice-cold water for 5 minutes. Drain; pat dry.

2. Shave off corn kernels with a sharp knife, leaving them attached to each other, if possible. Place into a large serving bowl. Add snap peas, mangoes, scallions, and basil.

3. **Dressing:** Combine dressing ingredients in a glass jar; seal tightly and shake well.

4. Add dressing to salad. Toss gently to combine. Cover; refrigerate until shortly before serving time.

Norene's Notes

- Variation: Instead of mangoes, use nectarines or peaches. Canned or frozen corn (lightly steamed) will also work well in this salad.
- No maple syrup? Replace with honey.

This salad was inspired by one of my closest childhood friends, Dori Weiss. Great all year round, it will keep well for about three days in the refrigerator.

Marvelous Marinated Salad

pareve · gluten-free · yields 6 servings

Ingredients

2 cans (15 oz/425 g each) baby corn, cut into 1-inch pieces

2 cans (14 oz/400 g each) sliced hearts of palm, drained and rinsed

1 pint (2 cups) cherry tomatoes, halved

½ small red onion, quartered and thinly sliced

¼ cup chopped fresh basil

Dressing

⅓ cup extra virgin olive oil

⅓ cup rice vinegar

2 cloves garlic, minced (about 1 tsp)

1 tsp dried tarragon

kosher salt

freshly ground black pepper

Method

1. In a large bowl, combine corn with hearts of palm, tomatoes, onion, and basil.

2. **Dressing:** Combine dressing ingredients in a glass jar; seal tightly and shake well.

3. Add dressing to salad; toss gently to combine.

4. Cover; refrigerate until serving time.

Norene's Notes

- Variation: For an Asian flavor, add 2 Tbsp soy sauce or tamari, 2 Tbsp honey, and 1 tsp toasted sesame oil to the dressing. Replace tarragon with 1 Tbsp fresh chopped basil.

Every Shabbos, my good friend Emily Hershtal makes this delicious kale salad. We call it her "everything salad" because it combines just the right amount of salty, crunchy, and sweet for a satisfying mouthful.

Everything Kale Salad

pareve • gluten-free • yields 10 servings

Ingredients

2 medium sweet potatoes, peeled and diced

1-2 Tbsp olive oil

kosher salt

freshly ground black pepper

1 medium bunch kale (about 1 lb/500 g)

1 pkg (16 oz/500 g) shredded green cabbage (about 4 cups)

¾ cup chopped dried figs

¾ cup dried blueberries or cranberries

1 cup pomegranate seeds

3 scallions, trimmed and thinly sliced

1 cup candied or toasted pecans (optional)

Dressing

⅓ cup extra virgin olive oil

⅓ cup balsamic vinegar

2 Tbsp pure maple syrup

2 Tbsp honey

2 tsp Dijon mustard

pinch salt

Method

1. Preheat oven to 400°F. Line a rimmed baking sheet with parchment paper.

2. Spread sweet potatoes in a single layer on prepared baking sheet. Drizzle with oil; sprinkle with salt and pepper. Bake, uncovered, for 35-40 minutes, until golden and tender.

3. Meanwhile, wash and dry kale. Remove and discard tough stalks and center veins. Tear into bite-sized pieces. Massage kale with your fingertips until leaves have wilted, about 5 minutes (see Norene's Notes, below).

4. Place kale into a large serving bowl. Top with sweet potatoes, cabbage, dried figs, dried blueberries, pomegranate seeds, and scallions. Cover; refrigerate.

5. **Dressing:** Combine dressing ingredients in a glass jar; seal tightly and shake well. Refrigerate until serving time.

6. Toss dressing with salad shortly before serving. Top with candied nuts, if using.

Norene's Notes

- Variation: Instead of kale, use Swiss chard (red or green) or arugula. Instead of cabbage, use shredded Brussels sprouts.
- Take a massage. A 5-minute massage transforms kale from bitter and tough to silky and sweet. After 4 to 5 minutes, taste it; if it's still bitter, massage it a bit longer. Some people massage kale with olive oil and salt to tenderize it. That's also O-Kale!

This staple salad is about two things: healthy greens and spicy, crunchy chickpeas. If you love the roasted chickpea recipe in my first book, then you'll also love this new spin. Roasted chickpeas pair perfectly with the tahini dressing.

Kale & Roasted Chickpea Salad

pareve · gluten-free · yields 8-10 servings

Ingredients

1 can (19 oz/540 ml) chickpeas, rinsed, drained, and patted dry

1 Tbsp olive oil

¾ tsp kosher salt

¼ tsp black pepper

½ tsp garlic powder

½ tsp sweet paprika

1 medium bunch kale (about 1 lb/500 g)

3 scallions, thinly sliced

Tahini Dressing

½ cup tahini paste

½ cup lemon juice (preferably fresh)

2 Tbsp water

1 Tbsp extra virgin olive oil

2 cloves garlic, minced (about 1 tsp)

pinch salt

Method

1. Preheat oven to 400°F. Line a rimmed baking sheet with parchment paper.

2. In a medium bowl, toss chickpeas with olive oil, salt, pepper, garlic powder, and paprika. Stir well.

3. Spread chickpeas in a single layer on prepared baking sheet. Bake, uncovered, for 35-40 minutes, until golden and crunchy, stirring occasionally. Cool completely. (See Norene's Notes, below.)

4. Meanwhile, wash and dry kale. Remove and discard tough stalks and center veins. Massage kale with your fingertips until leaves have wilted, about 5 minutes (see Norene's Notes, page 70). Chop kale into bite-sized pieces.

5. Place kale into a large serving bowl; add scallions. Cover; refrigerate.

6. **Tahini Dressing:** Combine dressing ingredients in a glass jar; seal tightly and shake well. Refrigerate until serving time.

7. Toss dressing with salad shortly before serving. Top with roasted chickpeas.

Norene's Notes

- Variation: Substitute canned lentils for chickpeas. Baking time is the same.
- Store roasted chickpeas or lentils in an airtight container at room temperature. So delicious!

This nostalgic salad takes me back to my childhood. I love it when such a simple recipe surprises you with such fabulous flavor. Perfect for guests when you're short on time.

Marinated Artichoke Salad

pareve • gluten-free • yields 8 servings

Ingredients

2 jars (12 oz/340 g each) marinated artichoke hearts

2 cans (14 oz/398 ml each) sliced hearts of palm

2 cans (15 oz/425 g each) baby corn

½ red onion, halved and sliced

Dressing

⅓ cup extra virgin olive oil

⅓ cup white vinegar

2 tsp honey

½ tsp salt

½ tsp garlic powder

pinch cayenne pepper

Method

1. Pour artichoke hearts and hearts of palm into a large colander. Drain well; do not rinse, as the spices will add flavor to the salad. Transfer to a large serving bowl.

2. Drain and rinse baby corn; cut into 1-inch pieces. Add to serving bowl along with onion.

3. Add dressing ingredients; mix well. Cover; refrigerate until serving time.

Norene's Notes

- Jarred marinated artichokes are a perfect pantry staple. They are great as a pizza topping or a delicious addition to salads and pasta dishes. Frozen artichokes also work well in this recipe. Thaw and pat dry before using.

- Homemade Marinated Artichokes: In a large jar, combine juice of 1 lemon and 2 Tbsp extra virgin olive oil. Add ¾ tsp salt, ¼ tsp pepper, and 1 tsp Italian seasoning. Seal; shake well. Rinse and drain 1 can (14 oz/398 ml) artichoke hearts (don't use frozen ones, since they are not spiced). Cut into quarters; add to jar. Reseal; shake well. Chill.

Adding fruits to vegetable dishes is one of my unique trademarks. A bit unusual but always satisfying, the combination of crunchy veggies with a splash of sweet, juicy fruit makes dishes like this berry-cabbage slaw bright, fresh, and flavorful.

Blueberry Cabbage Slaw

pareve • passover option • gluten-free • yields 8 servings

Ingredients

2 pkgs (16 oz/500 g each) sliced red cabbage (about 8 cups)

4 scallions, thinly sliced

2 cups fresh blueberries

¾ cup toasted pumpkin or sunflower seeds

Dressing

⅓ cup extra virgin olive oil

⅓ cup seasoned rice vinegar (see Norene's Notes, below)

2 Tbsp honey

kosher salt

freshly ground black pepper

Method

1. In a large serving bowl, combine cabbage and scallions.

2. **Dressing:** Combine dressing ingredients in a glass jar; seal tightly and shake well.

3. Pour dressing over cabbage mixture; toss well. Cover; refrigerate until serving time.

4. Stir in blueberries and pumpkin seeds shortly before serving. Adjust seasonings to taste.

Norene's Notes

- No seasoned rice vinegar? Use regular rice vinegar and boost the seasonings to make up for the lack of salt and sugar.
- Passover Option: Substitute lemon juice for rice vinegar; omit seeds.
- Drained canned pineapple tidbits or mandarin oranges are a nice switch-up for blueberries.
- Blueberries, pumpkin seeds, and sunflower seeds are part of a brain-healthy diet and help to preserve memory. Just remember to put them into your shopping cart!

One Mother's Day, my husband Jeffery brought me a beautiful bouquet of white hydrangeas with bright fuchsia and delicate pink peonies. I recreated that bouquet in this rosy-hued salad, dedicated to all the mothers out there who love to be pampered on their special day.

Mother's Day Cabbage Salad

pareve • gluten-free • yields 8 servings

Ingredients

2 pkgs (16 oz/500 g each) shredded green cabbage (about 8 cups)

6 radishes, trimmed and diced (do not peel)

3 scallions, trimmed and thinly sliced

2 cups strawberries, trimmed and thinly sliced

1 cup pomegranate seeds

¾ cup dried cranberries

Dressing

½ cup extra virgin olive oil

⅓ cup apple cider vinegar

3 Tbsp orange juice (preferably freshly squeezed)

2 Tbsp honey

¼ cup poppy seeds

kosher salt

freshly ground black pepper

Method

1. In a large serving bowl, combine cabbage, radishes, and scallions.

2. **Dressing:** Combine dressing ingredients in a glass jar; seal tightly and shake well.

3. Pour dressing over cabbage mixture; toss well. Cover; refrigerate until serving time.

4. Shortly before serving, add strawberries, pomegranate seeds, and dried cranberries to the bowl. Toss to combine.

Norene's Notes

- Nutrient-packed poppy seeds are believed to enhance brain function and boost the immune system. To help increase your fiber and mineral intake, add them to smoothies, salad dressings, and baked goods (e.g., cookies, cakes, muffins, breads).

- Store poppy seeds tightly closed in a cool, dark cupboard. You can also refrigerate or freeze them. They will keep for about 2 years.

One vegetable, two colors! Toss diced green and yellow zucchini with mushrooms for an easy side dish that pairs perfectly with most meals. Mushrooms offer a meaty texture and really absorb the tangy dressing, creating a burst of flavor.

Two Toned Zucchini & Mushroom Salad

pareve · gluten-free · yields 6-8 servings

Ingredients

2 yellow zucchini, ends trimmed, diced (do not peel)

2 green zucchini, ends trimmed, diced (do not peel)

½ lb/ 250 g shiitake mushrooms, trimmed and sliced (about 3 cups)

4 scallions, trimmed and thinly sliced on the diagonal

½ cup chopped fresh flat-leaf parsley

Dressing

⅓ cup extra virgin olive oil

⅓ cup lemon juice (preferably fresh)

2 Tbsp honey

1 Tbsp Dijon mustard

1 tsp kosher salt

freshly ground black pepper

Method

1. In a large serving bowl, toss zucchini with mushrooms, scallions, and parsley. Cover with a paper towel; refrigerate. (This prevents the salad from becoming soggy.)

2. **Dressing:** Combine dressing ingredients in a glass jar, seal tightly and shake well. Refrigerate until shortly before serving time.

3. Toss salad with dressing; adjust seasonings to taste. Serve chilled.

Norene's Notes

- Variation: if you can't find yellow zucchini, replace with 2 diced yellow bell peppers.
- Don't eat large quantities of raw button, cremini, or portobello mushrooms, as they contain small amounts of toxins, including some that are considered carcinogens. However, shiitakes have anti-viral and anti-cancer effects, so they are fine to eat raw.
- Remove shiitake mushroom stems as they are somewhat tough and chewy. Instead of throwing them out, wrap them in a paper towel and refrigerate. They will stay fresh for 1-2 days. Add to soups for added flavor. Discard stems after cooking.

My mom used to make this dish for us every week. She called it her "healthy potato salad," replacing starchy spuds with cauliflower florets and adding bell peppers and radishes for color. This simple, year-round salad is great for weekend meals and barbeques.

Cauliflower Salad

pareve • passover • gluten-free • yields 4-6 servings

Ingredients

1 medium head cauliflower, cut into small florets

1 red bell pepper, diced

1 orange bell pepper, diced

6 red radishes, trimmed and diced

4 scallions, trimmed and thinly sliced

Dressing

½ cup mayonnaise (light or regular)

1-2 tsp kosher salt

freshly ground black pepper

Method

1. Bring a large pot of lightly salted water to a boil. Add cauliflower florets; reduce heat and simmer for 6-8 minutes, until tender-crisp. Cooking time depends on the size of the florets — don't overcook. Drain well.

2. Place florets into a bowl of ice-cold water for 5 minutes. Drain well; pat dry.

3. Place florets, peppers, radishes, and scallions into a large bowl. Add dressing ingredients; toss to combine. Amount of mayonnaise and salt will depend on the size of the cauliflower.

4. Cover and refrigerate. Serve chilled.

Norene's Notes

- For tips on buying, storing, and prepping cauliflower, see Norene's Notes on page 50.
- Cauliflower emits an unpleasant smell when overcooked. Cook just until tender-crisp to minimize the odor.
- Don't cook cauliflower in an aluminum or iron pot, as the cauliflower will become discolored.

I'm a huge fan of onions. They're the "cherry on top" of every dish, whether it's a protein, or in this case, a healthy, balsamic-based spinach salad. With the addition of candied cashews and avocado, this salad is the ideal mix of sweet, creamy, and savory.

Balsamic Spinach Salad
with caramelized onions

pareve • passover • gluten-free • yields 8 servings

Ingredients

1 Tbsp extra virgin olive oil

1 large onion, halved and sliced

1 lb/500 g (about 10 cups) baby spinach (see Norene's Notes, below)

1 pint (about 2 cups) cherry tomatoes, halved

1 firm ripe avocado

¾ cup candied cashews or almonds (optional)

Dressing

⅓ cup extra virgin olive oil

¼ cup balsamic vinegar

2 Tbsp honey

1 Tbsp minced fresh thyme leaves (or **1 tsp** dried)

kosher salt

freshly ground black pepper

Method

1. Heat oil in a frying pan over medium-high heat. Add onion; sauté for 5-7 minutes, or until golden. Let cool to room temperature.

2. In a large serving bowl, combine spinach and tomatoes with sautéed onions. Cover; refrigerate.

3. **Dressing:** Combine dressing ingredients in a glass jar; seal tightly and shake well. Refrigerate until serving time.

4. Shortly before serving, peel, pit, and dice avocado. Toss salad with avocado and dressing. Sprinkle with nuts, if using.

Norene's Notes

• Preparation: Wash spinach thoroughly before using. Trim if necessary. Place into a large bowl of room-temperature water; swish the leaves around with your hands to dislodge any dirt or sand. Remove leaves, empty the bowl, refill with clean water, and repeat 2-3 times until all sand has been washed away. Dry thoroughly in a salad spinner. Triple-washed packaged spinach is very convenient — ready when you are.

In a last-minute recipe rush, I whipped together this pink and orange salad to take to my mom's for the weekend. To my surprise and delight, it was a big hit! My mom and sister went crazy for this sweet and juicy dish. Love those pomegranates around Rosh Hashanah time!

Pomegranate & Persimmon Salad

pareve • passover • gluten-free • yields 6 servings

Ingredients

8 cups arugula or mixed salad greens

3 scallions, thinly sliced

1 cup pomegranate seeds

2 firm (Fuyu) persimmons, thinly sliced

¾ cup toasted sliced almonds

Dressing

⅓ cup extra virgin olive oil

⅓ cup pomegranate juice

3 Tbsp balsamic vinegar

2 Tbsp honey

1 clove garlic, minced (about ½ tsp)

kosher salt

freshly ground black pepper

Method

1. In a large bowl, combine arugula with scallions, pomegranate seeds, and persimmons. Cover; refrigerate.

2. **Dressing:** Combine dressing ingredients in a glass jar; seal tightly and shake well.

3. Gently toss salad with dressing and almonds just before serving.

Norene's Notes

- No persimmons? Substitute nectarines or fresh apricots. No pomegranate seeds? Substitute dried cranberries.
- Fuyu persimmons are round, crisp, and squat; they can be eaten like apples. Hachiya persimmons are oblong, soft, and pulpy; they are used in baking. Store persimmons stem-end down at room temperature.
- This dressing is wonderful on any leafy salad greens, or as a marinade for chicken, meat, or fish.
- To seed a pomegranate, score around the middle of the pomegranate, but don't cut through. Twist to separate pomegranate into two halves. Invert one half over a bowl, seeds facing down. Tap the top firmly with a wooden spoon to release seeds into the bowl. Discard white pith. Repeat with the other half. Seeds will keep 2-3 days in the refrigerator.

This colorful salad was inspired by my good friend, Amiee Hass. I've always admired Amiee's creativity in the kitchen and couldn't help but love the look of bowtie pasta tossed with bright green spinach.

Spinach Pasta Salad
with mandarins & dried cranberries

pareve • gluten-free option • yield 8 servings

Ingredients

2 cups uncooked bowtie pasta (see Norene's Notes, below)

1 lb/500 g (about 10 cups) baby spinach

¾ cup dried cranberries

1 can (11 oz/312 g) mandarin oranges, rinsed and drained

½ cup candied slivered or whole almonds (optional)

Dressing

⅓ cup extra virgin olive oil

⅓ cup rice vinegar

2 Tbsp soy sauce or tamari

2 Tbsp honey

2 tsp toasted sesame oil (optional)

2 cloves garlic, minced (about 1 tsp)

½ tsp onion powder

pinch salt

Method

1. Cook pasta in boiling salted water according to package directions. Drain well, pat dry, and let cool.

2. In a large serving bowl, combine spinach, dried cranberries, mandarin oranges, and cooled pasta. Cover; refrigerate.

3. **Dressing:** Combine dressing ingredients in a glass jar; seal tightly and shake well. Refrigerate until serving time.

4. Gently toss salad with dressing just before serving. Sprinkle with slivered almonds, if using.

Norene's Notes

- Variations: Use any pretty shape of pasta, gluten-free or regular. Different every time!
- Instead of candied almonds, use toasted almonds (slivered or sliced).
- Using Your Noodle: If you cook the whole package of pasta, use the leftovers for a quick lunch for your kids — or yourself. Just add tomato sauce and a sprinkling of grated cheese; heat in the microwave until the cheese melts.

The beauty of the new fruits at our Rosh Hashanah celebration inspired me to get creative. Admiring the bright colors, various shapes, and juicy textures in the exotic-fruit section of my grocery store, I decided to try something new with the golden-yellow star fruit.

Strawberry Star Fruit Salad

pareve • passover • gluten-free • yields 8 servings

Ingredients

8 cups mixed salad greens

1 pint (about 2 cups) strawberries, hulled and sliced

2 star fruits, thinly sliced

¼ cup diced red onion

½ cup chopped candied pecans

Dressing

⅓ cup olive oil

⅓ cup apple cider vinegar

2-3 Tbsp honey

kosher salt

freshly ground black pepper

Method

1. In a large serving bowl, combine mixed greens with strawberries, star fruit, and onion. Cover; refrigerate.

2. **Dressing:** Combine dressing ingredients in a glass jar; seal tightly and shake well. Refrigerate until serving time.

3. Gently toss salad with dressing just before serving. Sprinkle with candied pecans.

Norene's Notes

- Variation: Substitute 1 diced mango or 2 nectarines for star fruit. Use orange or mango juice instead of apple cider vinegar.
- Star fruit, also known as carambola, is native to Indonesia and Sri Lanka. When cut crosswise, the slices form five-pointed stars. Star fruit is completely edible, including its skin, with a texture similar to grapes. If overripe, star fruit is bland and soggy. If unripe, it is firm and sour.
- Star fruit makes a beautiful garnish for beverages, sorbets, and most fruit desserts.

Bring the traditional bean salad into the modern era by using non-traditional ingredients such as poppy seeds and sprouts. Luscious and slightly sweet, the poppy seed dressing makes the flavors really pop. It's a perfect dish for large parties, picnics, and potlucks.

Four Bean Salad
with poppy seed dressing

pareve · dairy option · gluten-free · yields 8 servings

Ingredients

1 lb/500 g green (or a mix of green and yellow) beans, ends snapped off

1 can (19 oz/540 ml) red kidney beans or black beans, drained and rinsed

1 can (19 oz/540 ml) chickpeas, drained and rinsed

2 cups bean sprouts

Poppy Seed Dressing

⅓ cup extra virgin olive oil

⅓ cup seasoned rice vinegar

2 cloves garlic, minced (about 1 tsp)

3 Tbsp honey

3 Tbsp poppy seeds

1 tsp kosher salt

freshly ground black pepper

Method

1. Bring a large saucepan of salted water to a boil. Add green beans; boil for 3-5 minutes, until tender-crisp. Drain well. Place in a bowl of ice-cold water for a few minutes to shock them and help preserve their color. Drain well; pat dry.

2. In a large bowl, combine green beans, kidney beans, and chickpeas. Add dressing ingredients; toss to combine. Cover; refrigerate until shortly before serving time.

3. Stir in bean spouts at serving time. Adjust seasonings to taste.

Norene's Notes

- Dairy Variation: Top with 1 cup crumbled feta cheese at serving time. If desired, add ¼ cup minced fresh dill.
- Bean Cuisine: Beans and other legumes are excellent sources of protein and fiber and are gluten-free. They help to lower cholesterol and control blood glucose, help prevent cancer and heart disease, and promote good digestive health.

Fish

In my kitchen, "delicious" never has to mean complicated or time consuming. Quick to make and perfect for busy weeknights, this marinated fish makes the most out of your pantry staples. You can throw this together without breaking a sweat!

Honey Garlic Herbed Salmon

pareve · gluten-free · freezes well · yields 4-6 servings

Ingredients

4-6 salmon fillets
(about 6 oz/180 g each)

¼ cup soy sauce or tamari

2 Tbsp rice vinegar

2 Tbsp olive oil

3 Tbsp honey

4 cloves garlic, minced
(about 2 tsp)

2 tsp dried basil

2 tsp dried parsley

freshly ground black pepper

Method

1. Line a rimmed baking sheet with foil; coat with nonstick cooking spray. Arrange salmon in a single layer on prepared baking sheet.

2. In a small bowl, stir together soy sauce, rice vinegar, oil, honey, garlic, basil, parsley, and pepper.

3. Pour sauce evenly over fish; let stand for 20 minutes. Preheat oven to 425°F.

4. Bake, uncovered, for 12-15 minutes, basting occasionally, until salmon is glazed and golden. Serve hot or at room temperature.

Norene's Notes

- Variation: Instead of honey, substitute pure maple syrup or brown sugar. Instead of rice vinegar, use lemon juice.
- Double Up! Since this dish is also delicious cold, make a double batch and serve it over salad greens the next day.

This is one of my new favorites to serve my company. Easy and elegant, the crunchy cashew topping adds an extra layer of richness to this flaky pink fish. As long as there aren't any nut allergies at the table, this is a guaranteed hit.

Candied Cashew Salmon

pareve · passover · gluten-free · yields 6-8 servings

Ingredients

1 skinless boneless fillet of salmon or salmon trout (about 2 lb/1 kg)

kosher salt

freshly ground black pepper

3 Tbsp apricot jam

1 cup candied cashews (see Norene's Notes, below)

Method

1. Preheat oven to 425°F. Line a rimmed baking sheet with parchment paper.

2. Place salmon onto prepared baking sheet. Sprinkle generously with salt and pepper. Spread apricot jam evenly over salmon.

3. Using a food processor or mini prep, process cashews until coarsely chopped. Do not over-process. Sprinkle nuts over salmon.

4. Bake, uncovered, for 15-18 minutes, or until salmon flakes easily when pierced with a fork.

Norene's Notes

- Candied Cashews: Combine ¼ cup water and 1 cup sugar in a medium saucepan. Bring to a boil over medium heat. Stir in 3 cups cashews, salted or unsalted. Cook, stirring often, until liquid has evaporated and nuts have turned a deep golden brown. Spread on a parchment-lined baking sheet. When cool, break apart any clusters. Store in an airtight container for up to 2 weeks or freeze. Also delicious as a topping for mashed sweet potatoes or squash, and when added to salads! Almonds also work well in this recipe.

At the end of a busy week, I wasn't looking for anything too complicated and I didn't want to dirty too many dishes. Light, flavorful, and full of color, you wouldn't guess this was a last-minute meal. This multiplies easily, so it's great for guests!

One-Dish Salmon, Mushrooms & Peppers

pareve · gluten-free · do not freeze · yields 4-6 servings

Ingredients

4-6 salmon fillets
(about 6 oz/180 g each)

2-3 cups button mushrooms, trimmed
(do not slice)

8-12 assorted baby bell peppers, trimmed, cored

kosher salt

freshly ground black pepper

1-2 Tbsp olive oil

2-3 Tbsp honey

2-3 Tbsp soy sauce or tamari

Method

1. Preheat oven to 400°F. Line a rimmed baking sheet with parchment paper.

2. Arrange salmon, mushrooms, and whole peppers in a single layer on prepared baking sheet.

3. Sprinkle with salt and pepper; drizzle lightly on all sides with oil, honey, and soy sauce.

4. Bake, uncovered, for 15-18 minutes, or until salmon flakes easily when pierced with a fork. Transfer to a serving platter to serve.

Norene's Notes

- Variation: Instead of salmon, try arctic char, black cod, or salmon trout. Add 1 large zucchini, sliced on the diagonal, along with the peppers and mushrooms.
- Leftovers? Use as a topping for salad greens for lunch the next day.

You don't see salmon and red pepper together very often, but I promise you, it's phenomenal! The roasted pepper and raw scallion bring a mix of color and texture that presents beautifully. Buy the peppers prepared, or if you have time, roast them yourself.

Roasted Red Pepper Salmon

pareve · passover · gluten-free · freezes well · yields 6-8 servings

Ingredients

6-8 salmon fillets
(about 6 oz/180 g each)

kosher salt

freshly ground black pepper

½ tsp chili flakes (optional)

1 tsp onion powder

1 tsp garlic powder

1 cup jarred roasted
red peppers, drained, cut
into long strips

3 scallions, thinly sliced,
for garnish

Method

1. Preheat oven to 425°F. Line a rimmed baking sheet with foil; coat with nonstick cooking spray.

2. Arrange salmon in a single layer on prepared baking sheet. Sprinkle on both sides with salt, pepper, chili flakes, onion powder, and garlic powder.

3. Place pepper strips over salmon.

4. Bake, uncovered, for 12-15 minutes, until salmon flakes easily when pierced with a fork. Serve hot or at room temperature. Garnish with scallions.

Norene's Notes

- Variation: This recipe works well with other fish fillets (e.g., halibut, turbot, sole, pickerel, salmon trout). If using thinner fish fillets, reduce the cooking time accordingly.
- Easy Elegance: Arrange pepper strips in a tic-tac-toe design over fish before baking.

Salmon is one of my favorite proteins to cook because it's essentially a vessel for flavor and it's quick and easy to prepare. Every year I experiment with new taste and texture combinations. This simple and sophisticated recipe is delicious and also multiplies well for a crowd!

Basil Salmon
with sun-dried tomatoes

pareve · passover · gluten-free · do not freeze · yields 4-6 servings

Ingredients

1 skinless, boneless fillet of salmon (about 2 lb/1 kg) or 4-6 fish fillets

kosher salt

freshly ground black pepper

½ cup chopped fresh basil

¾ cup thinly sliced sun-dried tomatoes

2 Tbsp honey

1 cup coarsely crushed candied almonds (optional; see Norene's Notes, page 98)

Method

1. Preheat oven to 425°F. Line a rimmed baking sheet with foil; coat with nonstick cooking spray.

2. Place salmon onto prepared baking sheet. Sprinkle generously with salt and pepper.

3. In a medium bowl, stir together basil, sun-dried tomatoes, honey, and almonds, if using.

4. Spread mixture evenly over salmon.

5. Bake, uncovered, for 15-18 minutes, or until salmon flakes easily when pierced with a fork. Serve hot or at room temperature.

Norene's Notes

- Sun-dried tomatoes are often oil-packed. If so, save the oil and add it to your favorite salad dressing. If they are not oil-packed, soak them briefly in hot water to plump them.
- An easy way to slice sun-dried tomatoes is to cut them with kitchen shears!

A humble fish dish with bold, tangy flavors, this is a great option for relaxed lunches and dinners. Not wanting to overwhelm this mild fish with too many flavors, I paired it with pickled red onions. Once pickled, the onions turn a brilliant magenta that's beautiful against the white fish.

Pan-Fried Fillets & Pickled Onions

pareve · gluten-free · freezes well · yields 4-6 servings

Ingredients

Pickled Onions

½ cup water

½ cup apple cider vinegar

2 Tbsp honey

1 tsp kosher salt

1 small red onion, halved, thinly sliced

Fish

2 Tbsp grapeseed oil

4-6 fish fillets, such as halibut, tilapia, turbot, pickerel, or sole (about 6 oz/180 g each)

kosher salt

freshly ground black pepper

¼ cup chopped fresh dill, for garnish

Method

1. **Pickled Onions:** Combine water, vinegar, honey, and salt in a medium saucepan; bring to a boil. Stir in onion slices. Remove from heat; let cool.

2. **Fish:** In a large nonstick skillet, heat oil over medium-high heat. Season fillets generously with salt and pepper. Fry fillets 4-5 minutes per side, or until just cooked through.

3. Transfer fish to a platter; spoon on pickled onions. Garnish with dill. Serve hot or at room temperature.

Norene's Notes

- Side dish suggestion: This sautéed spinach is great with any fish dish: Heat 1 Tbsp grapeseed oil in a large skillet or wok over medium-high heat. Add 6 cups baby spinach leaves and 1 Tbsp minced garlic. Stir-fry for 3-4 minutes, just until spinach has wilted. Season with salt and pepper..

The flavors are perfectly balanced and the presentation is so beautiful. Parchment paper seals in the flavorful juices, and the fish comes out silky and tender, with a bright aroma of parsley, tomatoes, and lemon. Halibut and black cod will work nicely, too.

Lemon Sea Bass in Parchment Packets

pareve · passover · gluten-free · freezes well · yields 4-6 servings

Ingredients

4-6 sea bass fillets
(about 6 oz/180 g each)

kosher salt

freshly ground black pepper

2 cloves garlic, minced
(about 1 tsp)

½ cup chopped fresh parsley

1 cup cherry tomatoes,
halved

1 lemon, thinly sliced

juice of **1** lemon

Method

1. Preheat oven to 400°F. Cut four to six large squares of parchment paper. Prepare a large rimmed baking sheet.

2. Place a fillet on each sheet of parchment; season generously with salt and pepper. Top with garlic, parsley, tomatoes, and lemon slices. Squeeze lemon juice evenly over fish.

3. Seal parchment packets by crimping edges tightly closed with your fingers. Place onto prepared rimmed baking sheet. (Can be prepared a few hours ahead of time and refrigerated.)

4. Bake for 15-18 minutes.

5. **To serve:** Transfer each packet to individual plates. Carefully open them at the table, being careful not to be scalded by the hot steam.

Norene's Notes

- Variation: Add 2-3 Tbsp chopped fresh dill or basil for a different flavor.
- Instead of individual packets, place assembled fillets in an even layer in individual parchment cooking bags. Seal tightly and place onto a rimmed baking sheet. Bake as directed. Use a wide spatula to transfer packets to a large serving platter.

This dish packs an incredible amount of flavor considering it has so few ingredients. The layering technique infuses the fish with flavor throughout the cooking process, and as the tomatoes break down, they provide a simple sauce for the fish.

Roasted Tomato Fish Fillets

pareve · passover · gluten-free · do not freeze · yields 6 servings

Ingredients

2 firm, ripe beefsteak tomatoes, trimmed and sliced about ½-inch thick

kosher salt

freshly ground black pepper

4 cloves garlic, minced (about 2 tsp), divided

6 fish fillets, such as tilapia, turbot, pickerel, or sole (about 6 oz/180 g each)

1 cup chopped fresh basil leaves

2 Tbsp olive oil

Method

1. Preheat oven to 400°F. Coat the bottom and sides of a 9 x 13-inch baking dish with nonstick cooking spray.

2. Arrange a layer of sliced tomatoes in the prepared baking dish. Sprinkle with salt, pepper, and half the garlic.

3. Arrange fish fillets over tomatoes; top with basil. Sprinkle with salt, pepper, and remaining garlic. Drizzle with olive oil.

4. Bake, uncovered, for 10-12 minutes, until fish flakes easily when pierced with a fork. Serve hot or at room temperature

Norene's Notes

- Tilapia fillets have a thicker side and a thinner side. For even cooking, cut each fillet in half lengthwise, making two long pieces. Next, cut the thick piece in half through the center. You will now have three long pieces that are all about the same thickness.

Roasted garlic is well worth the wait! The caramelization takes the bite out of the garlic, resulting in smooth, creamy cloves that are sweet and rich. It's a simple rustic dish that serves beautifully every time.

Garlic & Tomato Fish Fillets

pareve · passover · gluten-free · freezes well · yields 4-6 servings

Ingredients

2 heads garlic, separated into cloves, peeled (see Norene's Notes, below)

1 pint cherry tomatoes

kosher salt

freshly ground black pepper

1-2 Tbsp olive oil, for drizzling

4-6 turbot, halibut, sole, or tilapia fillets (about 6 oz/180 g each)

2 tsp chopped fresh thyme leaves

additional thyme leaves, for garnish

Method

1. Preheat oven to 400°F. Line a rimmed baking sheet with parchment paper.

2. Spread garlic cloves and tomatoes on prepared baking sheet. Sprinkle with salt and pepper; drizzle with oil. Roast, uncovered, for 20 minutes.

3. Remove pan from oven. Push garlic and tomatoes to the side. Arrange fish fillets in a single layer in the pan. Sprinkle with salt, pepper, and thyme.

4. Bake fish together with garlic and tomatoes for an additional 12-15 minutes.

5. Transfer to a serving platter; garnish with additional thyme leaves.

Norene's Notes

- An average head of garlic contains about 15 cloves. You can also buy peeled garlic cloves in bulk.
- Variation: Roast baby potatoes, halved, in the oven at the same time as the fish (Step 2). When the fish is ready, dinner is done!
- Sea bass or black cod also work well in this recipe.

An almond-meal coating and pretty chive garnish put an upscale spin on classic fish sticks. Crispy on the outside with a warm, flaky fish center, this dish is still fun for kids but great for adults too. Serve with your favorite dipping sauce.

Almond-Crusted Fish Sticks

pareve · passover · gluten-free · freezes well · yields 4-6 servings

Ingredients

2 Tbsp olive oil

1 cup almond flour (finely ground almonds)

2 Tbsp sweet paprika

1 tsp kosher salt

freshly ground black pepper

4-6 firm fish fillets, such as salmon or halibut (about 6 oz/180 g each)

½ cup creamy Caesar salad dressing (bottled or homemade), optional

Method

1. Preheat oven to 425°F. Line a rimmed baking sheet with parchment paper.

2. Place olive oil into a shallow bowl. In a second medium shallow bowl, stir together almond flour with paprika, salt, and pepper until well combined.

3. Cut fish into 3-inch strips.

4. Dip fish sticks into oil; then dredge them in almond flour mixture, coating all sides. Arrange in a single layer on prepared baking sheet.

5. Bake, uncovered, for 10-12 minutes, or until fish flakes easily when pierced with a fork. Serve hot or at room temperature. Use Caesar dressing as a dipping sauce, optional.

Norene's Notes

- Variation: Instead of dipping fish sticks into oil in Step 4, dip into Caesar dressing, then in almond flour mixture.

- Make your own almond meal: Place blanched almonds into a food processor or mini prep. Process with quick on/off pulses to start, then process just until fine. Processing time will depend on whether you used whole, slivered, or sliced almonds. Do not over-process or you will end up with almond butter!

Coated with bold spices and finished with a squeeze of fresh lime, these fillets are packed with knock-out flavors. Most of the ingredients are probably in your kitchen already — pick up some fish and make it tonight! If you want more heat, add an extra pinch of cayenne.

Chili Lime Fish Fillets

pareve · passover · gluten-free · freezes well · yields 6-8 servings

Ingredients

2-3 Tbsp olive oil

2 Tbsp dried parsley

2 tsp sweet paprika

1 tsp dried oregano

1 tsp garlic powder

1 tsp onion powder

¼ tsp chili powder

¼ tsp cayenne pepper
(or to taste)

½ tsp kosher salt

¼ tsp freshly ground
black pepper

6-8 fish fillets,
such as tilapia, turbot,
pickerel, or sole
(about 6 oz/180 g each)

juice of **2** limes
(see Norene's Notes, below)

Method

1. Preheat oven to 425°F. Line a baking sheet with parchment paper.

2. Place olive oil into a shallow bowl. In a second wide shallow bowl, stir together parsley, paprika, oregano, garlic powder, onion powder, chili powder, cayenne pepper, salt, and pepper until well combined.

3. Dip fish fillets into oil; then dredge them in seasoning mixture, coating both sides. Arrange fillets in a single layer on prepared baking sheet.

4. Bake, uncovered, for 10-12 minutes, or until fish flakes easily when pierced with a fork.

5. Just before serving, squeeze lime juice over fish. Serve hot or at room temperature.

Norene's Notes

- Lime-Aid: Lime zest also makes a great garnish. Before you juice the limes, use a zester or the small holes on a box grater to remove zest from the fruit. To avoid pesticides, organic fruit is best. Always wash and dry limes well before zesting them. For maximum flavor, zest limes just before using.

Poultry

Salsa & Grilled Chicken
Tomato Olive Salsa

- meat
- passover
- gluten-free
- chicken freezes well
- yields 6 servings

Ingredients

Salsa

1 cup pitted black olives, halved

1 cup cherry tomatoes, halved

¼ cup diced red onion

2 cloves garlic, minced (about 1 tsp)

¼ cup minced fresh parsley

1 tsp dried oregano

3 Tbsp extra virgin olive oil

3 Tbsp orange juice

1 Tbsp honey

Grilled Chicken

6 single boneless, skinless chicken breasts (or **12** boneless, skinless thighs)

kosher salt

freshly ground black pepper

2 cloves garlic, minced (about 1 tsp)

1 tsp dried oregano

¼ cup chopped fresh parsley

Mango Salsa

- meat
- passover
- gluten-free
- chicken freezes well
- yields 6 servings

Ingredients

Salsa

1 ripe mango, peeled, pitted, and diced

2 ripe peaches or nectarines, peeled, pitted, and diced

¼ cup diced red onion

2 Tbsp extra virgin olive oil

2 Tbsp lime juice

1 Tbsp brown sugar

2 Tbsp chopped fresh basil

Grilled Chicken

6 single boneless, skinless chicken breasts (or **12** boneless, skinless thighs)

kosher salt

freshly ground black pepper

¼ cup chopped fresh basil

Avocado Cucumber Salsa

- meat
- passover
- gluten-free
- chicken freezes well
- yields 6 servings

Ingredients

Salsa

3 baby cucumbers, trimmed and diced (do not peel)

¼ cup diced red onion

1 firm, ripe avocado, peeled, pitted, and diced

¼ cup chopped fresh mint

2 Tbsp extra virgin olive oil

2 Tbsp lime juice

1 Tbsp honey

kosher salt

freshly ground black pepper

Grilled Chicken

6 single boneless, skinless chicken breasts (or **12** boneless, skinless thighs)

kosher salt

freshly ground black pepper

¼ cup chopped fresh mint

Everyone loves salsas. They're fresh in flavor, crowd-pleasers, and an easy way to add fruits and vegetables to our diets. These colorful salsas are bursting with bright, refreshing flavors that will liven up any meal.

Method

1. **Salsa:** In a medium bowl, combine olives, tomatoes, red onion, garlic, parsley, and oregano. Add oil, orange juice, and honey. Mix gently to combine. Cover; refrigerate.

2. **Chicken:** Heat an indoor grill, setting it to medium-high.

3. Sprinkle chicken on all sides with salt, pepper, garlic, oregano, and parsley.

4. Grill chicken for 4-6 minutes per side, until grill marks appear and juices run clear.

5. Transfer chicken to a serving platter; top with salsa.

Method

1. **Salsa:** In a medium bowl, combine mango, peaches, and red onion. Add oil, lime juice, brown sugar, and basil. Mix gently. Cover; refrigerate.

2. **Chicken:** Heat an indoor grill, setting it to medium-high.

3. Sprinkle chicken on all sides with salt, pepper, and basil.

4. Grill chicken for 4-6 minutes per side, until grill marks appear and juices run clear.

5. Transfer chicken to a serving platter; top with salsa.

Method

1. **Salsa:** In a medium bowl, combine cucumbers, red onion, avocado, and mint. Add oil, lime juice, honey, salt, and pepper. Mix gently. Cover tightly, pressing plastic wrap directly against the salsa. Refrigerate until serving time.

2. **Chicken:** Heat an indoor grill, setting it to medium-high.

3. Sprinkle chicken on all sides with salt, pepper, and mint.

4. Grill chicken for 4-6 minutes per side, until grill marks appear and juices run clear.

5. Transfer chicken to a serving platter; top with salsa.

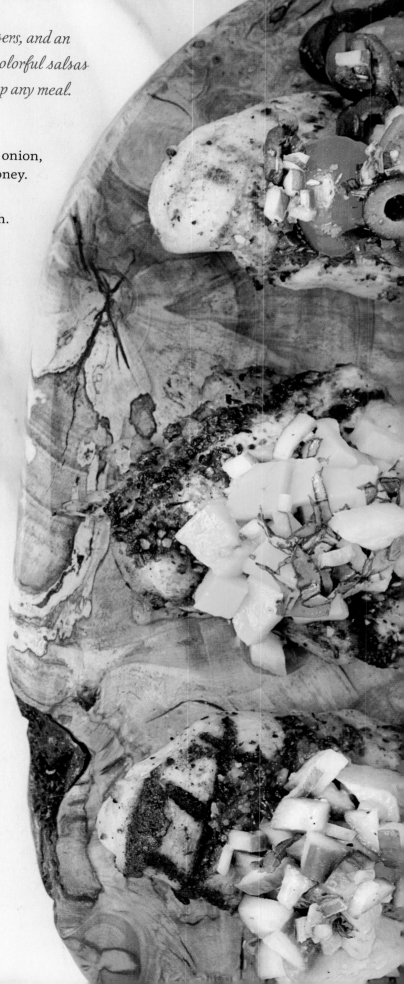

This fantastic chicken dish is packed with healthy goodness and takes no time at all to prepare. Each chicken packet is presented so beautifully — it's definitely a wow dish to show off to guests.

Chicken Packets
with spinach & peppers

meat · passover · gluten-free · freezes well · yields 6 servings

Ingredients

⅓ cup olive oil

zest and juice of **1** large lemon (about 2 tsp zest and ¼ cup juice)

4 cloves garlic, minced (about 2 tsp)

1 tsp kosher salt

¼ tsp black pepper

¼ cup chopped fresh parsley or dill

6 single boneless skinless chicken breasts or **12** boneless skinless thighs (about 2 lb/1 kg)

1 red bell pepper, halved and thinly sliced

1 yellow bell pepper, halved and thinly sliced

1 orange bell pepper, halved and thinly sliced

6 cups baby spinach, lightly packed

Method

1. Cut six pieces of parchment paper large enough to enclose chicken and vegetables. Prepare a rimmed baking sheet.

2. In a large bowl, whisk together olive oil, lemon zest, lemon juice, garlic, salt, pepper, and parsley. Add chicken and peppers. Mix well. Marinate for 20-30 minutes. (Can be prepared in advance and marinated overnight in the refrigerator. Bring to room temperature before assembling.)

3. Preheat oven to 400°F.

4. Place 1 cup spinach on each piece of parchment. Top with 1 chicken breast or 2 thighs and a mixture of bell peppers. Drizzle each portion lightly with remaining marinade.

5. Seal parchment by crimping edges closed with your fingers. Arrange packets in a single layer on a rimmed baking sheet.

6. Bake 25-35 minutes, depending on thickness of chicken breasts.

7. Place parchment packets on individual dinner plates. Carefully open them at the table, being careful not to burn yourself with the steam.

Norene's Notes

- Variations: Instead of lemon juice and zest, use lime or orange. Instead of bell peppers, use 2-3 cups diced zucchini, asparagus tips, and/or sliced mushrooms. Sprinkle with chopped thyme or rosemary.

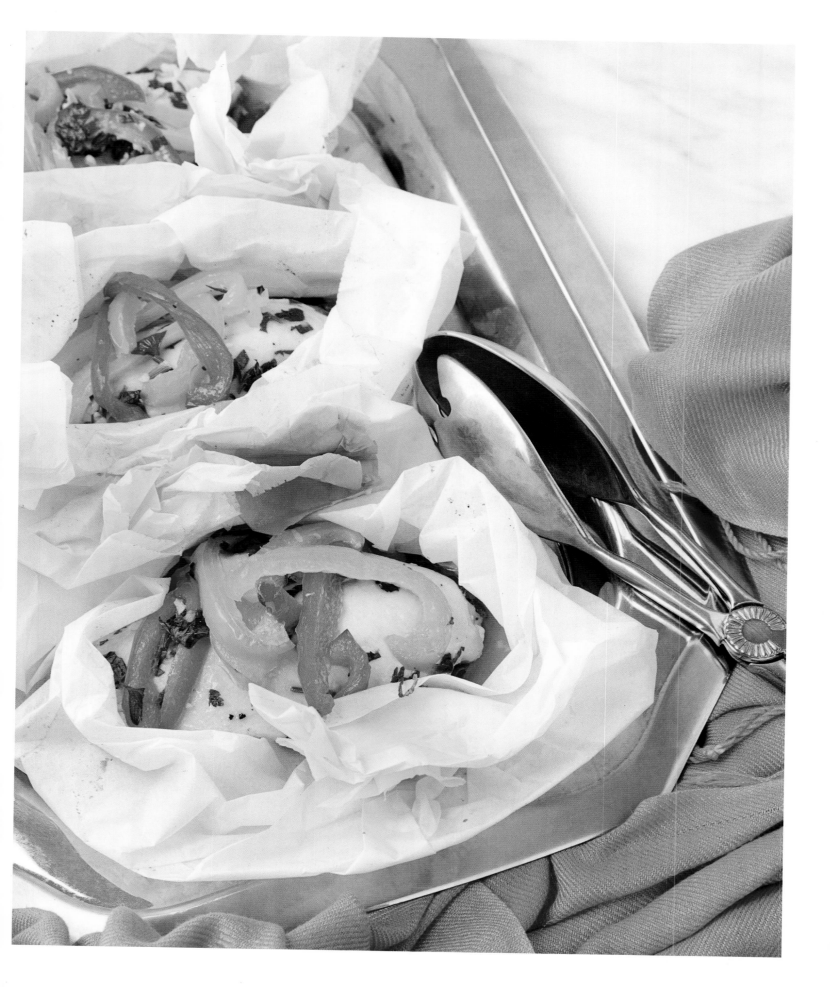

I had a house full of company the first time I prepared this chicken dish. Out of the oven, onto the table, it was so effortless and delicious that no one would believe I'd never made it before. You'll like how easy it is to make, and you'll love how no one can ever get enough!

Pesto Chicken

meat · passover · gluten-free · freezes well · yields 4-6 servings

Ingredients

6 single boneless skinless chicken breasts (or **12** boneless skinless thighs)

kosher salt

freshly ground black pepper

Pesto

2 cloves garlic

1 cup baby spinach

1 cup fresh basil leaves

1 tsp kosher salt

½ tsp black pepper

⅓ cup lemon juice (preferably fresh)

⅓ cup extra virgin olive oil

½ cup pine nuts, walnuts, almonds, or pumpkin seeds

Method

1. Preheat oven to 400°F. Line a rimmed baking sheet with parchment paper.

2. Sprinkle chicken on both sides with salt and pepper. Arrange in a single layer on prepared baking sheet.

3. **Pesto:** In a mini prep or food processor fitted with the "S" blade, process garlic, spinach, basil, salt, pepper, lemon juice, olive oil, and nuts until puréed, 12-15 seconds.

4. Spread pesto evenly over chicken, coating both sides. (Too much pesto? See Norene's Notes, below.) Marinate for 20 minutes, or overnight in the refrigerator if you have time.

5. Bake, uncovered, for 25-30 minutes, or until cooked through and juices run clear. Cooking time will depend on thickness of breasts. Serve hot or at room temperature.

Norene's Notes

- Too much pesto? Serve it as a topping for the cooked chicken or add it to your favorite salad dressing or dip. A spoonful or two in potato salad is also delicious.

- Pesto Pasta Primavera: Pesto is also amazing on any kind of cooked pasta, especially when combined with sautéed onions, mushrooms, red bell peppers, and asparagus. (You need ¼ cup pesto, 3 cups vegetables, and 1 pkg (12 oz/375 g) pasta cooked according to package directions.) For a creamier dish, add in a little rice milk or soy milk.

Hearty and heart-healthy, this quick dish is an ideal dinner option for busy weeknights, yet elegant enough for a light Shabbat lunch. It keeps you full when you're on the run and doesn't skimp on taste. Great for lunch the next day!

Chicken & Quinoa Salad

meat · passover · gluten-free · chicken freezes well · yields 8-10 servings

Ingredients

2 cups lightly salted water or chicken broth

1 cup quinoa, rinsed and drained

6 single boneless, skinless chicken breasts, cut into small chunks

kosher salt

freshly ground black pepper

½ tsp cayenne pepper (or to taste)

2 cloves garlic, minced

2 Tbsp grapeseed oil

4 cups baby spinach, coarsely chopped

2 stalks celery, diced

¾ cup dried cranberries

2 fresh apricots, diced

¼ cup extra virgin olive oil

3 Tbsp lemon juice (preferably fresh)

3 Tbsp honey

kosher salt

freshly ground black pepper

Method

1. Bring lightly salted water to a boil in a medium saucepan over high heat. Add quinoa; reduce heat. Simmer, covered, for 15 minutes, or until tender. Remove from heat; let stand for 10 minutes, covered. Fluff quinoa with a fork. Transfer to a large serving bowl.

2. In a large bowl, season chicken with salt, pepper, cayenne, and garlic; mix well.

3. Heat oil in a nonstick wok or large skillet over high heat. Stir-fry chicken pieces for 4-5 minutes, until cooked through. Cool slightly.

4. Combine quinoa with chicken, spinach, celery, dried cranberries, and apricots. Drizzle with oil, lemon juice, honey, salt, and pepper. Toss to combine. Serve immediately or serve chilled.

Norene's Notes

- Variation: Instead of baby spinach, use mixed salad greens. Instead of celery, use 2-3 baby cucumbers, thinly sliced. Instead of apricots, use peaches or nectarines.
- Vegetarian Version: Use diced firm tofu instead of chicken (but not on Passover!) or just omit the chicken.

This hearty, crunchy salad tops my list of slaw-style dishes. Passed through the skillful hands of so many home cooks, then to my friend Emily Hershtal, and finally to me, this versatile version has become a mainstay on my Shabbat table — and now it can be on yours.

Smoked Turkey Cabbage Slaw

meat · passover · gluten-free · do not freeze · yields 8 servings

Ingredients

2 bags (16 oz/500 g each) shredded green cabbage (about 8 cups)

2 stalks celery, thinly sliced

4 scallions, thinly sliced

1 cup dried cranberries

1 smoked boneless deli turkey breast (about 3 lb/1.4 kg), trimmed and diced

Dressing

⅓ **cup** vegetable oil

⅓ **cup** white vinegar

3 Tbsp honey or brown sugar

pinch salt

freshly ground black pepper

Method

1. In a large bowl, combine cabbage, celery, scallions, dried cranberries, and diced turkey. Cover; refrigerate.

2. **Dressing:** Combine dressing ingredients in a glass jar; seal tightly and shake well. Refrigerate.

3. Add dressing to cabbage mixture shortly before serving. Mix well. Serve chilled.

Norene's Notes

- Variations: Use a mixture of red and green cabbage. Instead of dried cranberries, substitute diced dried apricots. Add ½ cup diced red bell pepper.
- Slice Your Own: 1 large cabbage yields about 8 cups. Peel off and discard any tough outer leaves. Cut cabbage through the stem end into 4 pieces, then cut off and discard the hard white core. Slice cabbage crosswise into very thin slices. A food processor does it quickly.

Classic cranberry relish is great for the cooler months, but when the weather warms up, I like to accent my roasted turkey with the summery flavors of fresh strawberries and pineapple. This dish is perfect for holiday dinners — even on Passover!

Roast Turkey
with strawberry pineapple salsa

meat · passover · gluten-free · turkey freezes well · yields 8 servings

Ingredients

1 (about 4 lb/1.8 kg) boneless, skinless rolled or whole turkey breast

2 Tbsp olive oil

1 Tbsp sweet paprika

1 Tbsp garlic powder

1 Tbsp onion powder

½-1 tsp dried thyme

1 tsp kosher salt

1 tsp black pepper

½ cup water or chicken broth

Strawberry Pineapple Salsa

1 cup sliced strawberries

1 can (14 oz/397 g) whole cranberry sauce

1 cup fresh pineapple, diced

Method

1. Coat a large, heavy roasting pan with nonstick cooking spray.

2. Place turkey breast into prepared pan. Drizzle with olive oil; sprinkle with paprika, garlic powder, onion powder, thyme, salt, and pepper. Rub oil and seasonings into turkey on all sides. (If you have time, marinate it, covered, in the refrigerator for several hours or overnight.)

3. Preheat oven to 350°F. Pour water into the bottom of the roasting pan, being careful not to drizzle it over the seasoned turkey. Cover pan loosely with foil.

4. Roast turkey, covered, for 1½ hours. Uncover and roast 30 minutes longer, basting occasionally. Calculate 25-30 minutes per pound to determine total cooking time.

5. **Salsa:** Meanwhile, in a medium serving bowl, combine strawberries, cranberry sauce, and pineapple; stir to combine. Cover; refrigerate.

6. Remove turkey breast from oven and let stand, covered, for 15-20 minutes for easier slicing. Slice turkey about ½-inch thick (an electric knife makes it easier).

7. Transfer slices to a serving platter. Pour hot pan juices over turkey; serve salsa on the side.

Norene's Notes

- Variation: Use 1 can (14 oz/397 g) pineapple tidbits, well drained, instead of fresh.
- Test for Doneness: A meat thermometer inserted into the roasted turkey breast should register an internal temperature of 165-170°F.

A simple and fun way to use ground chicken! Even your kids will enjoy these burgers, and they don't have any preservatives. Prepare these at your next BBQ. Multiplies easily.

Grilled Chicken Burgers

meat · gluten-free · freezes well · yields 4 burgers

Ingredients

1 lb/500 g lean ground chicken

2 cloves garlic, minced (about 1 tsp)

½ cup minced fresh parsley

¼ cup diced red onion

¼ tsp chili powder

¼ tsp kosher salt

freshly ground black pepper

1 Tbsp soy sauce or tamari

oil, for brushing

Method

1. In a large bowl, combine ground chicken with garlic, parsley, onion, chili powder, salt, pepper, and soy sauce. Stir lightly to combine.

2. Shape chicken mixture into 4 burgers, wetting your hands for easier handling. Brush burgers lightly with oil on both sides.

3. Preheat grill to medium-high. Grill burgers 6-8 minutes per side, until cooked through.

Norene's Notes

- Sliders: Form chicken mixture into 8-10 mini burgers. Prepare and grill about 5 minutes per side. Serve on toasted mini rolls or buns with your favorite condiments (ketchup, mustard, relish, aioli, lettuce, tomatoes, onions, pickles).
- Thai Style Burgers: Replace chili powder with 1 tsp minced red chili pepper; replace parsley with cilantro. Add 1 tsp minced fresh ginger. Ground turkey can replace chicken.
- Watching your carbs? Wrap your burger in lettuce instead of bread.

Schnitzel is the ideal vehicle for creative flavors and textures. This is the perfect protein dish when you want something different. With a flaky, fresh herb coating, this unique version doesn't disappoint.

Flaked Quinoa Schnitzel

meat · passover · gluten-free · freezes well · yields 6 servings

Ingredients

6 boneless, skinless chicken breasts, pounded thin (or **12** boneless, skinless chicken thighs, butterflied)

kosher salt

freshly ground black pepper

2 eggs

1½ cups quinoa flakes

4 cloves garlic, minced (about 2 tsp)

2 Tbsp chopped fresh basil leaves

2 Tbsp chopped scallions

2 Tbsp chopped fresh parsley

1 Tbsp fresh lemon zest

oil, for frying

fresh basil, parsley, and lemon wedges, for garnish

Method

1. Lightly sprinkle chicken on both sides with salt and pepper.

2. In a medium bowl, lightly beat eggs. In a second medium bowl, combine quinoa flakes, garlic, basil, scallions, parsley, and lemon zest. Mix well.

3. Dip chicken first into egg, then dredge in quinoa mixture, coating all sides.

4. In a large nonstick skillet, heat oil over medium-high heat. Working in batches, fry chicken on both sides until cooked through and juices run clear, 3-5 minutes per side.

5. Pat chicken with paper towels to remove excess oil. Keep warm in an oven at 250°F, or transfer to a serving platter. Garnish with additional fresh herbs and lemon wedges.

Norene's Notes

- Quinoa flakes (dried quinoa that has been converted to a flaky texture similar to panko crumbs) is sold in boxes. The flakes are gluten-free, cholesterol-free, and an excellent source of protein and fiber. Buy them at your health food or bulk store.

As soon as my sister-in-law, Eden Litwack, mentioned her honey-sriracha chicken, I knew I had to create my own version. Spicy, succulent, and outside-the-box, this is a winning dish for those who like a spicy kick to their food. Thanks for the inspiration, Eden!

Honey Sriracha Chicken

meat · gluten-free · freezes well · yields 4-6 servings

Ingredients

1 chicken
(about 3 lb/1.4 kg),
cut into eighths

kosher salt

freshly ground black pepper

4 cloves garlic, minced
(about 2 tsp)

2 Tbsp vegetable oil

⅓ cup honey

1-2 Tbsp sriracha or hot
sauce (add more if you like it
super spicy)

2 Tbsp soy sauce or tamari

juice of **1** lime (about 2 Tbsp)

2 Tbsp toasted sesame
seeds, for garnish

Method

1. Coat a 9 x 13-inch baking dish with nonstick spray. Trim and discard excess fat from chicken pieces. Arrange chicken in a single layer, skin-side up, in prepared baking dish. Sprinkle on all sides with salt, pepper, and garlic.

2. In a medium bowl, combine oil, honey, sriracha, soy sauce, and lime juice. Mix well. Drizzle evenly over chicken, coating it on all sides. If you have time, marinate for 30 minutes or overnight in the refrigerator.

3. Preheat oven to 375°F.

4. Roast, uncovered, basting occasionally, for 1 hour and 15 minutes, or until chicken is cooked through, golden, and juices run clear.

5. Transfer chicken to a serving platter; garnish with sesame seeds.

Norene's Notes

- Sriracha is a hot sauce or chili sauce made from a paste of chili peppers, vinegar, garlic, sugar, and salt. It's often in the Asian aisle of your supermarket. If you can't find it, substitute hot sauce.
- Add sriracha to garlicky mayonnaise for a tasty dip. Sriracha adds a kick to salad dressings and sauces; it can also be used as a condiment at the table. Store opened bottle of sriracha in the refrigerator.

Bringing together some quintessential Italian flavors — basil, garlic, tomatoes, and red wine — this chicken is perfect for company. All you need to add is a simple side salad and some crusty bread (but not on Passover).

Red Wine Chicken & Potatoes

meat · passover · gluten-free · freezes well · yields 4-6 servings

Ingredients

1 chicken
(about 3 lb/1.4 kg),
cut into eighths

12 baby red potatoes,
scrubbed and halved
(do not peel)

kosher salt

freshly ground black pepper

6 cloves garlic, minced
(about 1 Tbsp)

1 cup red wine

3 Tbsp tomato paste

½ cup balsamic vinegar

¼ cup honey

½ cup chopped
fresh basil leaves

Method

1. Coat a 9 x 13-inch baking dish with nonstick cooking spray.

2. Trim and discard excess fat from chicken pieces. Arrange chicken in a single layer, skin-side up, in prepared baking dish. Add potatoes, tucking them between chicken pieces. Sprinkle chicken and potatoes with salt, pepper, and garlic.

3. In a medium bowl, combine wine, tomato paste, vinegar, honey, and basil. Mix well. Spoon sauce evenly over chicken and potatoes, coating all sides. If you have time, marinate for 1 hour, or overnight in the refrigerator.

4. Preheat oven to 375°F.

5. Roast, uncovered, basting occasionally, for 1 hour and 15 minutes, or until cooked through, glazed, and juices run clear.

Norene's Notes

- Variations: Instead of potatoes, use 2 cups squash cubes. Red wine vinegar works well, but may be difficult to find for Passover.

- If using boneless, skinless chicken breasts or thighs, reduce oven temperature to 350°F; bake, covered, for 30-40 minutes. Uncover and bake an additional 10 minutes.

When the sugar and spice of this simple chicken dish start to caramelize, a heavenly aroma floats through the house. Ground cinnamon adds unexpected warmth, and cinnamon sticks add a simple touch of elegance.

Maple Cinnamon Chicken

meat · gluten-free · freezes well · yields 4-6 servings

Ingredients

1 chicken (about 3 lb/1.4 kg), cut into eighths

2-3 large sweet potatoes, trimmed, halved, thinly sliced into half moons (do not peel)

3 shallots, trimmed and halved

3-4 cinnamon sticks

kosher salt

freshly ground black pepper

3 Tbsp brown sugar

1 tsp ground cinnamon

1 tsp dried thyme

3 Tbsp pure maple syrup

¼ cup water

Method

1. Preheat oven to 400°F. Coat a large roasting pan with nonstick spray.

2. Trim and discard excess fat from chicken pieces. Arrange chicken in a single layer, skin-side up, in roasting pan. Add sweet potatoes, shallots, and cinnamon sticks, tucking them between and around chicken pieces. Sprinkle generously with salt and pepper.

3. In a small bowl, combine brown sugar, cinnamon, and thyme. Stir well. Sprinkle mixture evenly over chicken and vegetables. Drizzle with maple syrup.

4. Add water to baking dish, being careful not to drizzle it over the seasoned chicken and vegetables.

5. Bake, uncovered, basting occasionally, for 1 hour and 15 minutes, or until juices run clear and chicken is glazed and golden. Transfer to a serving platter.

Norene's Notes

- Variation: Add 8-9 Medjool dates, halved and pitted, with vegetables.
- Sweet potatoes contain antioxidants, including beta-carotene, which converts to vitamin A in the body. The deeper the orange, the higher the beta-carotene content is. Sweet potatoes have a medium glycemic index (GI). One medium sweet potato contains about 6.6 grams fiber.

Sweet nectarines and fresh tarragon bring the beauty of the summer season to this simple chicken dish. The wine-based broth infuses the chicken with a slightly sweet, subtle flavor while keeping it moist and tender.

Nectarine Chicken

meat · passover · gluten-free · freezes well · yields 4-6 servings

Ingredients

1 chicken
(about 3 lb/1.4 kg),
cut into eighths

2-3 large nectarines,
quartered and pitted
(do not peel)

2 shallots, peeled and halved

kosher salt

freshly ground black pepper

3 Tbsp brown sugar

¾ cup sweet white wine

½ cup orange juice

¼ cup honey

6 sprigs fresh tarragon
or thyme

Method

1. Coat a 9 x 13-inch baking dish with nonstick spray.

2. Trim and discard excess fat from chicken pieces. Arrange chicken in a single layer, skin-side up, in prepared baking dish. Add nectarines and shallots, tucking them between chicken pieces. Sprinkle chicken, nectarines, and shallots with salt, pepper, and brown sugar.

3. In a medium bowl, combine wine, orange juice, and honey. Mix well. Drizzle evenly over chicken, nectarines, and shallots, coating all sides. Top with tarragon sprigs. If you have time, marinate for 30 minutes or overnight in the refrigerator.

4. Preheat oven to 375°F.

5. Roast, uncovered, basting occasionally, for 1 hour and 15 minutes, or until cooked through, golden, and juices run clear.

Norene's Notes

- Variation: No nectarines? Use plums, peaches, or apricots. Dried fruit (e.g., 1½ cups dried apricots, prunes, or nectarines) also works here.
- Wine adds flavor and will tenderize the chicken. After a dinner party, store leftover wine in the refrigerator to use in this recipe.

Sometimes all you really need is an easy chicken recipe. This is it! It's also perfect for kids when you're having lots of company. This is a great basic chicken sauce, so feel free to try it on cut-up chicken or boneless breasts (see Norene's Notes, below).

Yum Drums

meat · gluten-free · freezes well · yield 4-6 servings

Ingredients

12 chicken drumsticks or
2 dozen chicken wings

kosher salt

freshly ground black pepper

2 tsp sweet paprika

½ tsp powdered ginger

¼ cup honey

¼ cup ketchup

2 Tbsp soy sauce or tamari

4 cloves garlic, minced
(about 2 tsp)

2 scallions, thinly sliced on
the diagonal, for garnish

Method

1. Coat a 9 x 13-inch baking dish with nonstick cooking spray.

2. Trim and discard excess fat from chicken. Arrange chicken in a single layer in prepared dish. Sprinkle with salt, pepper, paprika, and ginger.

3. In a measuring cup, combine honey, ketchup, soy sauce, and garlic; mix well.

4. Drizzle mixture over chicken; marinate for 20-30 minutes or overnight in the refrigerator. Remove from refrigerator; bring to room temperature.

5. Preheat oven to 375°F.

6. Bake, uncovered, basting occasionally, for 45-55 minutes, until glazed. Transfer to a serving dish; garnish with scallions.

Norene's Notes

- Chunky Pineapple Chicken: Instead of drumsticks, use 4-6 boneless, skinless chicken breasts, cut into 1-inch chunks. Add 1 can (15 oz/425 g) pineapple chunks, drained, for the last 10 minutes of baking. Serve over rice or quinoa.

The essence of easy elegance, this foolproof recipe is a great option for entertaining, especially for the High Holidays. Some people don't eat nuts on Rosh Hashanah or are allergic to them; if so, omit pistachios and garnish the chicken with chopped fresh parsley for a burst of color.

Honey-Roasted Pistachio Chicken

meat · gluten-free · freezes well · yields 4-6 servings

Ingredients

1 chicken (about 3 lb/1.4 kg), cut into eighths

kosher salt

freshly ground black pepper

1 tsp garlic powder

Sauce & Topping

½ cup honey

¼ cup soy sauce or tamari

¼ cup ketchup

¼ cup brown sugar, lightly packed

3 cloves garlic, minced (about 1½ tsp)

¾ cup coarsely chopped pistachios

Method

1. Preheat oven to 375°F. Coat a 9 x 13-inch baking dish with nonstick spray.

2. Trim and discard excess fat from chicken pieces. Arrange chicken in a single layer, skin-side up, in baking dish. Sprinkle on all sides with salt, pepper, and garlic powder.

3. Roast, uncovered, for 55-60 minutes.

4. **Sauce:** In a medium bowl, combine honey, soy sauce, ketchup, brown sugar, and garlic. Mix well. Drizzle evenly over chicken. Sprinkle chicken with pistachios.

5. Roast uncovered, basting occasionally, for 15 minutes, until glazed.

Norene's Notes

- Honey has an indefinite shelf life. Store it at room temperature in a tightly closed container away from light. If honey crystallizes, just heat it over low heat and the sugar crystals will dissolve. You can also microwave it in a glass measuring cup for 30-60 seconds.

With gorgeous red bell peppers and a bold garlic flavor, this chicken dish contains a blend of basic Italian ingredients. I like to serve it over quinoa or mashed potatoes and smother it with any extra sauce. No one does simple elegance like the Italians.

Chicken Italiano

meat · passover · gluten-free · freezes well · yields 4-6 servings

Ingredients

6 single boneless, skinless chicken breasts (or **12** boneless, skinless thighs)

kosher salt

freshly ground black pepper

2-3 Tbsp grapeseed or vegetable oil

4 cloves garlic, minced (about 2 tsp)

1 large onion, chopped

2 red bell peppers, halved and thinly sliced

1 can (28 oz/796 ml) diced tomatoes with their liquid

juice of **1** lemon (about 3-4 Tbsp)

1 bunch fresh parsley leaves, chopped (about 1 cup), divided

Method

1. Lightly sprinkle chicken on both sides with salt and pepper.

2. In a large deep skillet, heat oil over medium heat. Working in batches, brown chicken for 4-6 minutes per side. Remove chicken from skillet; set aside.

3. Add garlic, onion, and bell peppers to skillet (no need to wash the pan first); sauté for 5-7 minutes, or until onions are softened.

4. Add diced tomatoes with their liquid, lemon juice, and half the parsley to skillet. Bring to a boil; reduce heat.

5. Add browned chicken to the skillet. Cover; simmer about 15 minutes, basting occasionally, until chicken is cooked through and juices run clear.

6. Garnish with remaining parsley.

Norene's Notes

- Whole Chicken Variation: Use 1 whole chicken, cut into eighths. Working in batches, brown chicken in a Dutch oven on medium heat for 5-7 minutes per side; remove from pan and set aside. Continue as directed above (Steps 3-6), but increase cooking time to 45-50 minutes.
- Variation: Use balsamic vinegar instead of lemon juice. Add your favorite Italian seasonings (e.g., basil, oregano, thyme).

Meat

With thin, easy-to-chew slices, skirt steak might be the best cut of beef to serve my kids, but it's not only for little mouths. Skirt steak has an intense, beefy flavor that is enjoyed by all ages.

Grilled Skirt Steak

meat • passover • gluten-free • freezes well • yields 4-6 servings

Ingredients

1 skirt steak
(about 2 lb/1 kg)

1 Tbsp olive oil

juice of **1** lemon (3-4 Tbsp),
preferably fresh

2 Tbsp honey

3 cloves garlic, minced
(about 1½ tsp)

¼ cup chopped fresh mint or
basil, plus more for garnish

Method

1. Cut skirt steak lengthwise into thin, narrow pieces.

2. In a medium bowl, combine oil, lemon juice, honey, garlic, and mint; mix well.

3. Add skirt steak; marinate for 30 minutes at room temperature.

4. Preheat grill or barbecue, setting it to medium-high.

5. Grill over indirect heat for 4-5 minutes per side, until grill marks appear and meat reaches desired doneness. (For medium, cook to an internal temperature of 145°F.)

6. Garnish with additional mint leaves.

Norene's Notes

- No grill? Soak skewers in water for 30 minutes, then thread on the steak and broil in your oven about 4 inches from the heat for 4-5 minutes per side.

- Variation: Add cubed red bell peppers and/or sliced mushrooms to the ends of each skewer.

- Skirt steak is marbled with fat, which makes it very juicy. Since it is very salty, don't add salt when seasoning the meat.

With its golden color and speckled grains, Dijon mustard embodies casual sophistication. I've softened its punchy flavor with maple syrup, creating a crave-worthy dish for family and friends. Serve this hot from the grill or cook ahead and serve slightly chilled for Shabbat lunch.

Maple Mustard London Broil

meat · gluten-free · freezes well · yields 6 servings

Ingredients

1 London broil
(about 2 lb/1 kg)

kosher salt

freshly ground black pepper

2 cloves garlic, minced
(about 1 tsp)

¼ cup grainy Dijon mustard

3 Tbsp pure maple syrup

1 Tbsp fresh thyme or
tarragon leaves

Method

1. Sprinkle meat with salt, pepper, and garlic. Rub to coat on all sides.

2. Preheat broiler. Spray broiling rack with nonstick spray; line bottom tray with foil.

3. In a small bowl, combine Dijon mustard with maple syrup and thyme. Set aside.

4. Broil meat for 8 minutes on the first side. Remove pan from oven; turn meat over. Spread with Dijon mixture.

5. Return meat to oven; broil for an additional 7-8 minutes, or until meat reaches desired doneness. (For medium, cook to an internal temperature of 145°F.)

6. Let meat rest for 5 minutes. Slice against the grain, on the diagonal, into thin slices. Serve hot or at room temperature.

Norene's Notes

- You Go Grill! To use an indoor or outdoor barbeque, spread meat on both sides with mustard mixture. Marinate for 30 minutes while grill is preheating. Grill meat for 7-8 minutes per side.

- Leftovers? Add to your favorite salad the next day or make sandwiches on crusty rolls with leafy salad greens, sliced tomatoes, and onions.

I'm always looking for a new Friday night main that will surprise guests and look pretty on the table. This delicious dish is one of my latest favorites. What's not to love about a beautiful cut of marinated beef, smothered in a rich, savory mushroom sauce? It's simple and elegant.

Portobello London Broil

meat · gluten-free · freezes well · yields 6 servings

Ingredients

1 London broil
(about 2 lb/1kg

kosher salt

freshly ground black pepper

4 cloves garlic, minced
(about 2 tsp)

3 Tbsp brown sugar

⅓ cup soy sauce or tamari

¼ cup red wine vinegar

3 Tbsp olive oil

1 lb/500 g portobello
mushrooms, trimmed,
halved, and sliced

Method

1. Place London broil into a large resealable plastic bag. Sprinkle on both sides with salt and pepper. Add garlic, brown sugar, soy sauce, vinegar, and oil. Massage meat with marinade, then add mushrooms; massage gently. (See Norene's Notes, below.)

2. Marinate for 1 hour or overnight in the refrigerator.

3. Preheat broiler or grill. If broiling, spray broiling rack with nonstick spray; line bottom tray with foil.

4. Remove London broil from marinade and place on broiler rack or grill. Pour mushrooms and marinade into a medium saucepan.

5. Broil or grill meat for 8-10 minutes per side or until meat reaches desired doneness. (For medium, cook to an internal temperature of 145°F.)

6. Let meat rest for 5 minutes. Slice against the grain on the diagonal, into thin slices. Transfer to a serving platter; cover to keep warm.

7. Meanwhile, bring mushrooms and marinade to a boil. Reduce heat; simmer for 4-5 minutes. Pour heated sauce over London broil before serving.

Norene's Notes

- Take care not to break the sliced mushrooms when massaging them with the marinade!
- If you don't have Portobello mushrooms, use button mushrooms or a mixture of wild mushrooms.

I decided to challenge myself by creating a stripped-down rib dish that was bursting with flavors yet was not covered in sauce. A ginger, honey, and soy marinade was the perfect solution. Sweet yet spicy, the marinade breaks down the meat fibers.

Asian Flavored Miami Ribs

meat · gluten free · do not freeze · yields 4-6 servings

Ingredients

12 Miami beef ribs

⅓ cup soy sauce or tamari

⅓ cup balsamic vinegar (see Norene's Notes, below)

2-3 Tbsp honey

4 cloves garlic, minced (about 2 tsp)

2 Tbsp toasted sesame oil

1 Tbsp minced ginger

1 tsp cayenne pepper

1 tsp black pepper

sesame seeds, for sprinkling

Method

1. Place beef ribs into a large resealable plastic bag. Add soy sauce, vinegar, honey, garlic, sesame oil, ginger, cayenne, and pepper. Massage mixture into ribs, coating them on all sides. Seal tightly; marinate for up to 12 hours in the refrigerator. Turn bag over once or twice so marinade covers meat completely.

2. Remove bag from refrigerator one hour before cooking. If broiling, spray broiling rack with nonstick spray; line bottom tray with foil.

3. Remove ribs from marinade; discard marinade. Arrange ribs in a single layer on broiler pan or grill pan. Sprinkle with sesame seeds.

4. Preheat grill pan or broiler to high. Broil or grill ribs for 4-5 minutes on the first side. Turn ribs over; sprinkle again with sesame seeds. Broil or grill 4-5 minutes longer, depending on thickness of ribs and heat of your grill.

Norene's Notes

• Pineapple Miami Ribs: Use pineapple juice instead of balsamic vinegar in the marinade. In Step 2, after removing bag from refrigerator, add pineapple slices to marinade; marinate for 1 hour. Grill or broil pineapple slices along with the ribs. Crave-worthy!

• Miami ribs are thinly sliced, cross-cut short ribs/flanken. For maximum tenderness, marinate them for at least 12 hours and then cook on a very hot grill.

Whether you're cooking for Sunday afternoon football fans or mixing things up and serving breakfast-for-dinner, this deli hash is irresistible and loved by all — especially guys! What an easy way to capture the spirit of comfort food.

Deli Hash

meat · passover · gluten-free · do not freeze · yields 6 servings

Ingredients

6 medium potatoes, peeled and diced

1 lb/500 g button mushrooms, sliced

3 cups salami, diced into about ½-inch chunks

2 Tbsp olive oil

1 tsp sweet paprika

1 tsp garlic powder

1 tsp onion powder

½ tsp cayenne pepper (or to taste)

Method

1. Preheat oven to 400° F. Line a rimmed baking sheet with parchment paper.

2. In a large bowl, combine all ingredients; mix well.

3. Spread mixture in a single layer on prepared baking sheet.

4. Roast, uncovered, stirring occasionally, for 45-55 minutes, or until potatoes are crisp, golden, and fork-tender.

5. Transfer to a serving platter.

Norene's Notes

- Variation: Instead of potatoes, use 6 cups squash or sweet potato cubes. Some supermarkets sell them precut, which is very convenient. (Don't use frozen.) You could also use baby potatoes, halved.

- Serve this dish on rare occasions, as deli is not the healthiest choice — but boy, does it taste good!

My friends and readers know that I love adding the freshness of fruit to my dishes. Strawberries bring a pretty pop of color to these Miami ribs, while the garlic and onion in the glaze balance out the sweetness. Great any time of year, but especially in summer.

Balsamic Glazed Strawberry Ribs

meat · gluten-free · freezes well · yields 6 servings

Ingredients

12 Miami beef ribs

1 large onion, halved and sliced

2 cloves garlic, minced (about 1 tsp)

½ cup balsamic vinegar

½ cup strawberry jam

1 Tbsp water

1 cup diced fresh strawberries

Method

1. Coat a large roasting pan with nonstick cooking spray.

2. Arrange ribs over onion slices in a single layer in prepared pan.

3. In a small bowl, whisk together garlic, balsamic vinegar, strawberry jam, and water. Pour mixture over ribs.

4. Cover; marinate for 1 hour or up to 24 hours in the refrigerator.

5. Preheat oven to 350°F.

6. Bake, covered, 1½-2 hours, or until meat is tender. Baste occasionally.

7. Transfer to a serving platter; garnish with fresh strawberries.

Norene's Notes

- You can substitute regular flanken, which are a thicker cut of Miami ribs; just increase the cooking time to 3 hours. P.S. This dish is even better the next day!

- Change up this recipe by using apricot or mango jam; garnish with chopped dried apricots or dried mangoes.

I learned this excellent technique from our local butcher. The spice-rubbed ribs cook for three hours as the fabulous flavors are absorbed. During the last half hour of cooking, the ribs are smothered with barbecue sauce, giving them that perfect, restaurant-quality glaze.

Heavenly Spiced Ribs

meat · passover · gluten-free · freezes well · yields 8 servings

Ingredients

Spice Rub

1 Tbsp garlic powder

1 Tbsp onion powder

1 Tbsp sweet paprika

2 tsp kosher salt

1 tsp black pepper

8 beef short ribs (flanken)
(about 6 lb/2.7 kg)
(see Norene's Notes, below)

3 Tbsp olive oil

1 cup barbecue sauce

Method

1. **Spice rub:** In a medium bowl, combine garlic powder, onion powder, paprika, salt, and pepper.

2. Coat a large roasting pan with nonstick cooking spray.

3. Arrange short ribs in a single layer in prepared pan. Season ribs on all sides with spice rub; drizzle with oil. Marinate for 20-30 minutes.

4. Preheat oven to 350°F. Roast, covered, for 3 hours.

5. Remove pan from oven, uncover, and spread barbecue sauce evenly over ribs.

6. Roast, uncovered, for an additional 30 minutes or until glazed, basting occasionally.

Norene's Notes

- Variation: This recipe also works well with beef ribs (the rib bones from a prime rib).
- Do-Ahead: In Step 3, you can season the meat with the spice rub, cover, and refrigerate it up to a day or two before roasting.
- Slow Cooker Method: Prepare short ribs as directed in Steps 1-3, placing them into the sprayed insert of a slow cooker. Pour on barbecue sauce. Cook on low until tender, 8-10 hours.

I wanted to add a different twist to traditional corned beef— and nothing does that better than adding a handful of fresh herbs and a splash of lemon. The tangy pickled flavor of corned beef is the perfect match for those refreshing green herbs!

Corned Beef & Herbs

meat · passover · gluten-free · freezes well · yields 8 servings

Ingredients

4 lb/1.8 kg corned beef (pickled brisket) (1-2 briskets)

½ cup fresh parsley leaves, loosely packed

¼ cup fresh dill

¼ small red onion

2 cloves garlic (1 tsp minced)

2 Tbsp honey

juice of **½** lemon

pinch salt

freshly ground black pepper

Method

1. Bring a large pot of water to a boil. Rinse meat well under cold running water to remove excess spices. Add meat to pot; simmer, partially covered, for 2½ hours, or until fork tender. Drain and let cool. (Can be made up to a day in advance and refrigerated for easier slicing.)

2. Slice chilled meat across the grain into thin slices. Transfer to a serving platter (if serving cold) or to an ovenproof dish (if serving warm). Cover and refrigerate.

3. In mini prep or food processor, combine parsley, dill, onion, and garlic. Process with quick on/off turns, until coarsely minced. Add honey, lemon juice, salt, and pepper. Process briefly, just until combined. Transfer to a small bowl; cover and refrigerate.

4. Shortly before serving, either reheat corned beef or let stand at room temperature. Spoon or drizzle herb mixture over corned beef, or serve it on the side.

Norene's Notes

- Time It Right: Don't worry if your brisket isn't the size we call for in this recipe. Just adjust the cooking time accordingly. A good guideline is to simmer it for 35-45 minutes per pound, until fork tender.
- Brisket will slice best when chilled. An electric knife does a good job of making nice slices. Add broken bits to salads — or just nosh on them!

This colorful chilled salad is a creative way to add meat to Shabbat lunches without turning on the oven. The briny flavor of the beef is balanced by the sweet tanginess of the cranberries. Sophisticated and simple!

Green Bean & Corned Beef Salad

meat • gluten-free • meat freezes well • yields 6-8 servings

Ingredients

1 corned beef
(pickled brisket)
(about 3 lb/1.4 kg)

1 lb/500 g green beans,
halved, ends trimmed

4 scallions, thinly sliced

1 cup dried cranberries

Dressing

⅓ cup olive oil

⅓ cup red wine vinegar

2 Tbsp honey

1 Tbsp Dijon mustard

2 cloves garlic, minced
(about 1 tsp)

kosher salt

freshly ground black pepper

Method

1. Bring a large pot of water to a boil. Rinse meat well under cold running water to remove excess spices. Add meat to pot; simmer, partially covered, for 2½ hours, or until fork tender. Drain well, let cool, and refrigerate. (Can be made up to a day in advance for easier slicing.)

2. Bring a medium pot of lightly salted water to a boil. Add green beans; cook for 5-6 minutes, until tender-crisp (do not overcook). Drain well and immediately rinse under ice-cold water. Pat dry; place into a large serving bowl.

3. Slice chilled meat across the grain into ½-inch thick slices; then cut slices into 1-inch chunks. Add to green beans along with scallions.

4. **Dressing:** Combine dressing ingredients in a glass jar; seal tightly and shake well. Add to salad; toss gently to combine.

5. Shortly before serving, add cranberries, toss to combine, and serve.

Norene's Notes

- See Norene's Notes, p. 166, for more about beef cooking times.
- Short on Time? Buy a piece of pickled corned beef (or turkey breast) at your local deli and slice it as directed in Step 3.
- No red wine vinegar? Switch it up with lemon juice or rice vinegar.
- Corned beef tends to be salty, so you may prefer to soak it in cold water for about 30 minutes before cooking. Drain well; cook in fresh water.

Flavor-packed, these saucy ribs are an excellent choice for Shabbat or holiday dinners. I find that the key to melt-in-your-mouth meat is patience. Allow the full cooking time, and don't skimp on the wine.

Saucy Veal Spare Ribs

meat • gluten-free • freezes well • yields 4 servings

Ingredients

8 veal spare ribs
(about 3 lb/1.4 kg)

kosher salt

freshly ground black pepper

2 tsp sweet paprika

2 Tbsp grapeseed oil

2 large red onions,
coarsely chopped

6 cloves garlic, minced
(about 1 Tbsp)

2 tsp minced fresh thyme

2 cups red wine

¼ cup tomato paste

¼ cup soy sauce or tamari

⅓ cup honey

Method

1. Preheat oven to 350°F.

2. Place veal ribs into a large roasting pan coated with nonstick cooking spray. Sprinkle veal on all sides with salt, pepper, and paprika.

3. In a large saucepan, heat oil over medium-high heat. Add onions and garlic; sauté for 6-8 minutes, until tender. Stir in thyme, wine, tomato paste, soy sauce, and honey; bring to a boil. Reduce heat; simmer for 5 minutes.

4. Pour sauce over, around, and under veal.

5. Roast, covered, for 2 hours or until ribs are almost fork-tender. Uncover; baste well. Cook, uncovered, for an additional 30 minutes, until nicely glazed.

Norene's Notes

- This marinade works well on brisket, flank steak, or chicken. Wine acts as a tenderizer, creating melt-in-your-mouth meat.

Cannelloni noodles are a perfect vehicle for satisfying ingredients like beef, spinach, and my favorite, marinated hot peppers. The peppers add just the right amount of kick to keep guests wondering what your secret ingredient might be. I serve these with a leafy green salad.

Stuffed Beef Cannelloni

meat • gluten-free option • freezes well • yield 4-5 servings

Ingredients

2 Tbsp grapeseed oil

2 medium onions, diced

2 cloves garlic, minced (about 1 tsp)

1 lb/500 g lean ground beef (or ground turkey, chicken, or lamb)

½ tsp kosher salt

freshly ground black pepper

1 jar marinara sauce (about 3 cups)

½ cup marinated hot peppers, drained

¼ cup chopped fresh basil leaves

2 cups baby spinach leaves, chopped, plus additional for garnish, optional

1 pkg (250 g) oven-ready cannelloni tubes (regular or gluten-free) (not cooked)

Method

1. In a large nonstick wok or skillet, heat oil over medium heat. Add onions and garlic; sauté for 5 minutes, until onions are softened.

2. Add ground beef, salt, and pepper. Cook 8-10 minutes longer, stirring often, until beef is browned and no traces of pink remain.

3. Stir in marinara sauce, hot peppers, basil, and spinach. Cook 10 minutes longer, until thickened. Let cool completely.

4. Preheat oven to 350°F. Coat a 9 x 13-inch baking dish with nonstick cooking spray.

5. Scoop filling mixture into a large resealable bag. Seal tightly; snip off one corner of bottom of bag with scissors.

6. Squeeze the filling mixture into each cannelloni tube, filling them completely. Arrange in a single layer in prepared baking dish. Spoon any leftover filling mixture on top. (Can be prepared in advance and refrigerated.)

7. Bake, covered, for 35-45 minutes, until piping hot.

Norene's Notes

- When piping the filling into cannelloni tubes, fill them completely so that there are no air pockets.
- You can use a piping bag and pastry tube instead of a resealable bag.
- Never put hot filling into a plastic resealable bag!

A surprise show-stopper, these oversized meatballs are juicy, tender, and full of flavor. Smothered with a zesty, garlicky marinara sauce and served family-style on a large platter, this easy dish will make mouths water. Serve with crusty bread and a garden salad.

Massive Meatballs, Italian Style

meat • passover • gluten-free • freezes well • yields 12 large meatballs

Ingredients

Sauce

2 Tbsp olive oil

2 medium onions, diced

6 cloves garlic, sliced

2 jars (24 oz/680 g each) thick and zesty marinara sauce

1 tsp chili flakes (or to taste)

Meatballs

2 lb/1 kg lean ground beef (or chicken, turkey, or lamb)

1 tsp kosher salt

½ tsp black pepper

½ tsp chili flakes

1 Tbsp onion powder

1 Tbsp garlic powder

1 Tbsp sweet paprika

½ cup chopped fresh basil

Method

1. **Sauce:** Heat oil in a large pot over medium heat. Add onions and garlic; sauté for 5-6 minutes, until golden. Add marinara sauce and chili flakes; bring to a boil.

2. **Meatballs:** Meanwhile, in a large bowl, combine ground beef with salt, pepper, chili flakes, onion powder, garlic powder, and paprika. Mix lightly to combine. Do not over-mix or meatballs will be tough.

3. Form mixture into 2-inch round meatballs. (See Norene's Notes, below.) Add meatballs to sauce; shake pot back and forth gently so meatballs are covered with sauce.

4. Reduce heat; simmer, partially covered, for 1 hour. Shortly before serving, stir in basil.

Norene's Notes

• When shaping meatballs, wet your hands in cold water for easier handling. Many people prefer to use disposable gloves.

• Serve these meatballs over pasta, quinoa, or basmati rice. For a low-carb version, serve over spaghetti squash strands, or "zoodles," zucchini "noodles" made on a spiralizer.

Minimal prep and warm spices such as cumin and sweet paprika make this dish an easy but elevated option for weeknight dinners, especially in the fall. Roasted squash adds that deep comfort feel to the dish, while the pistachios bring a bit of texture. Best served over rice.

Spiced Beef
with roasted butternut squash

meat · passover · gluten-free · freezes well · yields 6 servings

Ingredients

1 butternut squash, peeled and cut into chunks (about 6 cups)

4 Tbsp olive oil, divided

kosher salt

freshly ground black pepper

2 large onions, diced

4 cloves garlic, minced (about 2 tsp)

1 lb/500 g lean ground beef (or chicken, turkey, or veal)

1 tsp sweet paprika

1 tsp turmeric

1 tsp cumin

½ cup chopped fresh parsley

½ cup chopped unsalted pistachios (optional)

Method

1. Preheat oven to 400°F. Line a rimmed baking sheet with parchment paper.

2. Arrange squash in a single layer on prepared baking sheet. Drizzle with 2 Tbsp oil; sprinkle with salt and pepper, coating all sides.

3. Roast, uncovered, for 45-50 minutes, or until glazed and golden.

4. Meanwhile, in a large skillet or wok, heat remainung oil over medium heat. Add onions and garlic; sauté for 5-7 minutes, until softened.

5. Add ground beef, paprika, turmeric, and cumin. Sprinkle with salt and pepper. Cook, stirring often, 8-10 minutes longer, until beef is browned and no traces of pink remain.

6. Transfer beef to a large serving bowl. Carefully stir in roasted squash and parsley. Garnish with pistachios, if using.

Norene's Notes

- Ground beef is generally made from lean meat and trimmings. I prefer a mix of 80% lean and 20% fat. The leaner the meat, the dryer it is.
- When browning ground meat in Step 4, stir it often or you'll end up with little meatballs instead of cooked ground meat!
- As a plated starter, serve this dish over a bed of rice or quinoa.

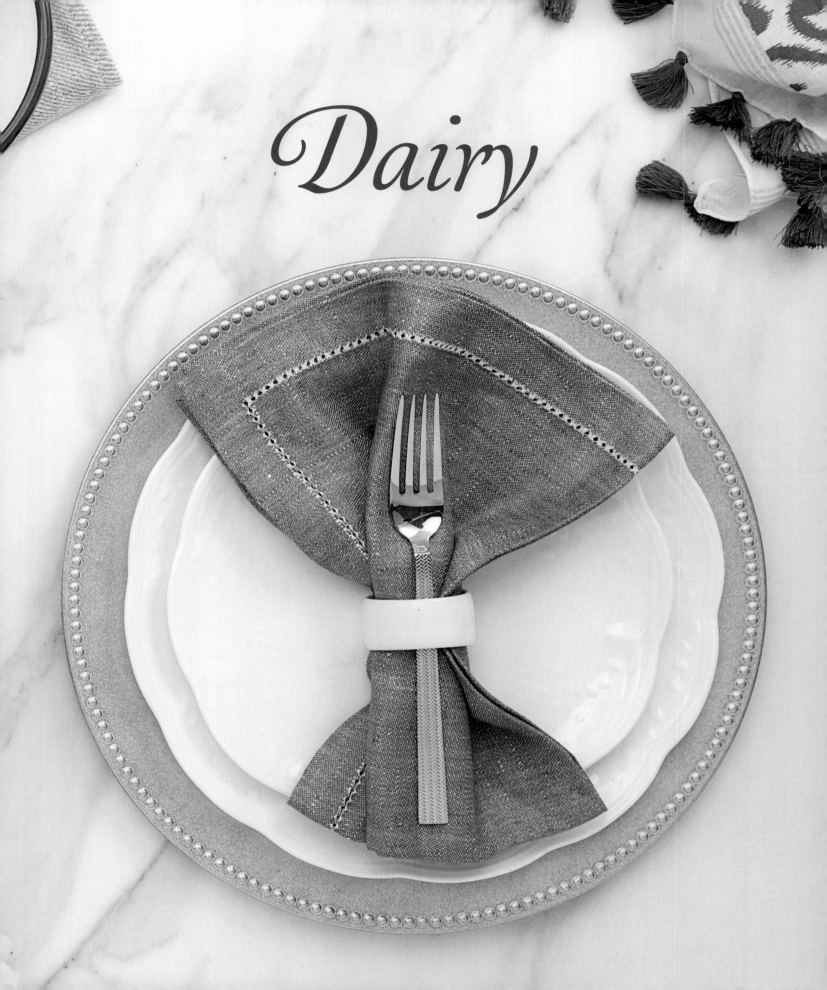

Dairy

Tangy, salty, and full of bright flavors. This lovely quinoa side dish is so simple to make. I came up with the recipe over Shavuot when I couldn't find the right mix of flavors to match my menu. This dish met that challenge and then some — it's a winner!

Italian-Style Quinoa
with sun-dried tomatoes & feta

dairy · passover · gluten-free · do not freeze · yields 8 servings

Ingredients

3 cups water

1½ cups quinoa, rinsed and drained

10-12 sun-dried tomatoes, chopped

½ cup chopped red onion

½ cup crumbled feta cheese

½ cup chopped fresh basil

toasted slivered almonds, for garnish (optional)

Dressing

⅓ cup extra virgin olive oil

⅓ cup lemon juice (preferably fresh)

kosher salt

freshly ground black pepper

Method

1. Bring water to a boil in a medium saucepan over high heat. Add quinoa; reduce heat. Simmer, covered, for 15 minutes or until tender. Remove from heat; let stand, covered, for 10 minutes. Fluff with a fork. Transfer to a large serving bowl; let cool.

2. Add sun-dried tomatoes, onion, feta cheese, and basil to quinoa. Drizzle in dressing ingredients; toss to combine. Cover; refrigerate until serving time.

3. Sprinkle with almonds before serving, if using.

Norene's Notes

- Variation: Use pine nuts instead of almonds.
- Rinse or Not? Some brands of quinoa do not require rinsing. When in doubt, follow package directions.
- If rinsing quinoa, always use a fine mesh strainer or the tiny seeds will fall through the holes. If you don't have a fine mesh strainer, line a regular strainer with a paper coffee filter.

Sometimes you need a little "fun" in the kitchen. These little individual quinoa pizzas are the perfect dish to serve to your kids or company. Packed with nutrients and veggies!

Quinoa Pizza Ramekins

dairy · passover · gluten-free · do not freeze · yields 12 servings

Ingredients

3 cups lightly salted water

1½ cups white or red quinoa

1 jar (24 oz) marinara sauce (about 3 cups)

3 cups pizza toppings (e.g., chopped mushrooms, bell peppers, onions)

2 cups shredded mozzarella cheese

½ cup grated Parmesan cheese

2 green onions, thinly sliced, for garnish

Method

1. Bring water to a boil in a medium saucepan over high heat. Add quinoa; reduce heat. Simmer, covered, for 15 minutes or until tender. Remove from heat; let stand for 10 minutes, covered. Fluff quinoa with a fork; let cool.

2. Preheat oven to 400°F. Coat 8 medium ovenproof ramekins with nonstick cooking spray; place on a rimmed baking sheet.

3. Spread about 2 Tbsp marinara sauce into each ramekin. Spoon about ¼ cup cooked quinoa into each ramekin; spread evenly. Top with veggies and mozzarella cheese. Repeat once more, beginning with quinoa and ending with cheese.

4. Bake, uncovered, for 20 minutes, or until cheese is golden and bubbly.

5. Remove from oven; sprinkle with Parmesan and green onions.

Norene's Notes

- No ramekins? Layer ingredients in a 7 x 11-inch baking dish coated with nonstick cooking spray, as directed above. Bake, uncovered, for 30-35 minutes, until golden and bubbly. Spoon onto individual serving plates.

These delicious cheese balls are packed with flavor and iron-rich greens, and they pair with just about everything. A cheesy alternative to toast, serve these with eggs for breakfast. They also make a hearty addition to tossed salads at lunch and are a delicious side dish for fish dinners.

Spinach Cheese Bites

dairy • passover option • gluten-free option • freezes well • yields 1 dozen

Ingredients

1 pkg (10 oz/300 g) frozen spinach, thawed, drained, squeezed dry (see Norene's Notes, below)

⅓ cup melted butter

1 small onion, finely diced

2 eggs

⅓ cup grated Parmesan cheese

½ cup shredded mozzarella cheese

½ tsp garlic powder

1 tsp kosher salt

¼ tsp pepper

1 cup unseasoned panko crumbs (gluten-free or regular)

Method

1. Line a rimmed baking sheet with parchment paper.

2. In a large bowl, combine spinach with butter, onion, eggs, cheeses, garlic powder, salt, pepper, and panko. Mix well.

3. Roll mixture into 1½-inch balls; place onto prepared baking sheet. Refrigerate for 20 minutes, while oven is preheating.

4. Preheat oven to 350°F. Bake for 25-30 minutes, until golden and piping hot. Serve hot or at room temperature.

Norene's Notes

- Thaw with Ease: A quick way to thaw frozen spinach is to microwave it in a glass bowl, covered, on high power, for 3 minutes.
- Variation: Instead of mozzarella, use Swiss or Cheddar cheese. If you like gooier bites, then double up on the shredded cheese.
- Passover Option: Use Passover panko, matzo meal, or cracker crumbs.
- Freeze with Ease: Mix and shape in advance, then freeze in a single layer. Transfer to a resealable plastic bag. When needed, bake frozen, adding 3-4 minutes to the baking time.

An old-school dish that deserves a comeback, this is light, fluffy, and best of all, versatile. Easy to tote to different events and excellent for lunch the next day! It's a great dish to serve on Shavuot or Chanukah.

Cheese Blintz Souffle

dairy · gluten-free option · freezes well · yields 8 servings

Ingredients

Batter

½ cup butter, melted and cooled

¼ cup sugar

2 eggs

¾ cup milk

1¼ cups flour (regular or gluten-free with xanthum gum)

1 tsp baking powder

½ tsp salt

ground cinnamon, for sprinkling

Filling

1½ lb/750 g farmers cheese (3 cups) (see Norene's Notes below)

2 cups cottage cheese (preferably small curd)

2 eggs

1 Tbsp sugar

1 Tbsp lemon juice (preferably fresh)

pinch salt

Method

1. Preheat oven to 325°F. Coat a 9 x 13-inch baking dish with nonstick cooking spray.

2. **Batter:** In a large bowl, combine butter, sugar, eggs, and milk; mix well. Add flour, baking powder, and salt; stir just until combined.

3. **Filling:** In a second large bowl, combine filling ingredients; mix well.

4. Spoon half the batter into prepared baking dish; spread evenly. Spoon filling evenly over batter. Top with remaining batter; spread evenly, using a rubber spatula. Sprinkle lightly with cinnamon.

5. Bake, uncovered, for 60-70 minutes, or until golden and set.

Norene's Notes

- What's in a Name? Farmers cheese may also be called pressed (dry) cottage cheese, depending on packaging.
- My late mom, Belle Rykiss, used to call this type of dish "puchadik," which means puffy and light as a feather. Dairy delicious!
- This dish is great topped with yogurt or sour cream and fresh berries.

I always love to prepare my potatoes in rounds — not because they are prettier than fries, but probably because I'm lazy! These are super pretty and with just a sprinkle of Parmesan, you have a wonderful dairy side dish.

Crispy Garlicky Parmesan Potatoes

dairy · passover · gluten-free · do not freeze · yields 6 servings

Ingredients

6 medium potatoes, well-scrubbed (do not peel)

3 Tbsp olive oil

4 cloves garlic, minced (about 2 tsp)

1 tsp kosher salt

freshly ground black pepper

½ tsp dried oregano

½ cup grated Parmesan cheese, divided

¼ cup thinly sliced chives

Method

1. Preheat oven to 400°F. Line two rimmed baking sheets with parchment paper.

2. Slice potatoes into ¼-inch rounds. Place into a large bowl; add oil, garlic, salt, pepper, and oregano. Sprinkle with Parmesan; mix well.

3. Arrange potato rounds in a single layer on prepared baking sheets.

4. Bake, uncovered, for 35-45 minutes, or until cheese is golden and bubbly.

5. Transfer to a large serving platter; garnish with chives. Serve immediately.

Norene's Notes

- Idaho potatoes (russets), which are baking potatoes, have thick skins and starchy interiors that become fluffy when cooked. Yukon Gold potatoes will also work nicely in this recipe. For even cooking, choose potatoes that are similar in size and shape.

- To prepare in advance, after cutting into rounds, soak potato slices in lots of cold water to prevent them from discoloring.

OK, gluten-free foodies, I have the perfect dish for you! This potato-crusted quiche has the delicate elegance of a traditional quiche, but with a crispy crust that might just be better than the original pastry version. Enjoy for brunches, lunches, and suppers. Perfect for Passover!

Potato-Crusted Quiche

dairy • passover • gluten free • freezes well • yields 6 servings

Ingredients

Crust

3 medium Idaho potatoes, peeled, cut into large chunks

1 medium onion, cut into large chunks

2 Tbsp vegetable oil

2 Tbsp potato starch

1 tsp kosher salt

freshly ground black pepper

Filling

2 cups fresh or frozen broccoli florets (thaw if frozen)

2 cups sliced mushrooms

½ tsp oregano

½ tsp garlic powder

1 tsp kosher salt

½ tsp black pepper

2 eggs

¼ cup milk

1 cup shredded Cheddar cheese

½ cup grated Parmesan cheese

Method

1. **Crust:** Preheat oven to 375°F. Coat the bottom and sides of a 10-inch glass or ceramic quiche dish with nonstick cooking spray.

2. In a food processor fitted with the shredding disk, shred potatoes and onions, using medium pressure.

3. Transfer mixture to a bowl; add oil, potato starch, salt, and pepper. Mix well.

4. Spoon mixture into prepared baking dish. Using the back of a spoon, spread mixture evenly, pushing it up the sides to form a crust. Bake, uncovered, 25-35 minutes, until golden.

5. **Filling:** In a large bowl, combine broccoli, mushrooms, oregano, garlic powder, salt, pepper, eggs, milk, and cheeses. Mix well.

6. Pour vegetable mixture into crust; spread evenly.

7. Return baking dish to oven. Bake 30-35 minutes longer, or until center is set. Let cool 5-10 minutes before cutting.

Norene's Notes

- No food processor? Use a box grater.
- Pan-tastic: Place quiche dish onto a parchment-lined rimmed baking sheet for easier transferring in and out of the oven and to catch spills.

Mac and cheese is the hallmark of comfort food. I've put a bit of a spin on this cheesy favorite by using orzo instead of elbow noodles, making it almost like a risotto-inspired mac and cheese. These little rice-shaped noodles give the dish a creamier texture.

Cheesy Orzo Mac & Cheese

dairy · freezes well · yields 6 servings

Ingredients

1 pkg orzo (12 oz/340 g)

1 Tbsp butter

1 cup milk
(low fat or regular)

2 cups shredded
Cheddar cheese

½ cup grated
Parmesan cheese

½ tsp kosher salt

freshly ground pepper

½ tsp dried thyme

Method

1. Cook orzo in salted water according to package directions. Drain well; return orzo to pot.

2. Add butter, milk, cheeses, salt, pepper, and thyme. Stir together until cheeses have melted.

3. Adjust seasonings to taste; garnish with additional thyme. Best served immediately.

Norene's Notes

- Mac and Cheese Gratin: Prepare orzo through Step 2, as directed above. Transfer mixture to a 9 x 13- inch baking dish coated with nonstick cooking spray. Sprinkle with ¾-1 cup panko or cornflake crumbs. Bake, uncovered, at 350°F for 25-30 minutes, until golden and bubbling.

- Company Coming? Transfer orzo mixture to individual ramekins; sprinkle with panko or cornflake crumbs. Place ramekins onto a rimmed baking sheet; bake for 15-20 minutes in a 350°F oven.

Everyone is always looking for that dairy salad — well, here's a beautiful one to impress your guests: simple and elegant, using lots of flavors, vegetables, and fruit.

Spinach, Mango & Mozzarella Salad

dairy · passover · gluten-free · do not freeze · yields 6 servings

Ingredients

6 cups baby spinach

1 medium head radicchio, trimmed, halved, thinly sliced

1 large ripe mango, peeled, pitted, thinly sliced

8 oz/250 g mozzarella cheese, cut into bite-sized chunks (about 2 cups)

1 cup chopped fresh basil leaves

Dressing

⅓ **cup** extra virgin olive oil

¼ **cup** balsamic vinegar

2 Tbsp honey

kosher salt

freshly ground black pepper

Method

1. In a large serving bowl, combine spinach with radicchio, mango, cheese, and basil. Cover; refrigerate.

2. **Dressing:** Combine dressing ingredients in a glass jar; seal tightly and shake well.

3. Add dressing to salad shortly before serving.

Norene's Notes

- Variations: Instead of radicchio, use 1 pkg (16 oz/500 g) shredded purple cabbage. Instead of mango, use 1-2 nectarines or peaches.

Once you try this dish, you may never want to eat asparagus any other way. Perfectly blanched crispy asparagus spears are tossed in a warm lemon-butter sauce — every bite is delicious. Simple and elegant, this dish is easy to double for company.

Lemon Butter Asparagus

dairy • pareve option • passover • gluten-free • yields 4 servings

Ingredients

1½ cups lightly salted water (approximately)

1 bunch asparagus (1 lb/500 g) (tough ends snapped off and discarded)

1 Tbsp olive oil

3 Tbsp salted butter (see Norene's Notes, below)

zest and juice of **1** lemon

¼ cup thinly sliced chives

Method

1. Heat water in a large, deep skillet until bubbling. Add asparagus; cook for 1-2 minutes, until tender-crisp. Drain asparagus; then place into a bowl of ice-cold water for 5 minutes. Pat dry.

2. Wipe skillet dry with a towel. Add oil, butter, lemon zest, and lemon juice; heat over low heat until butter has melted and sauce is piping hot.

3. Add asparagus and chives to skillet; toss with the sauce. Serve immediately.

Norene's Notes

- If you prefer to use unsalted butter, add salt to the finished dish.
- Pareve Option: Omit butter; increase olive oil to 3 Tbsp. (Note: Butter contains about 20% water, so you don't need to use the same amount of oil.) If desired, stir in 2 cloves of minced garlic along with the asparagus and chives.

These protein-packed parfaits are perfect for breakfast, and are fruity and sweet for a healthy dairy dessert treat. You can prepare all the ingredients in advance and assemble these parfaits at serving time.

Quinoa Granola Parfaits

dairy · gluten-free · quinoa freezes well · yields 4 servings

Ingredients

Granola

1 cup uncooked quinoa

¼ cup pumpkin seeds

¼ cup slivered almonds

¼ cup flax seeds

1 tsp ground cinnamon

¼ cup honey

2 Tbsp olive oil or grapeseed oil

½ cup dried cranberries

3 cups Greek yogurt

3 cups assorted fresh fruit (e.g., berries, cut-up figs, sliced banana)

Method

1. Preheat oven to 375°F. Line a rimmed baking sheet with parchment paper.

2. In a medium bowl, combine quinoa with pumpkin seeds, almonds, flax seeds, cinnamon, honey, and oil. Mix well.

3. Spread mixture evenly on prepared baking sheet. Bake for 10-15 minutes, until golden.

4. Let cool completely. Break into small, irregular pieces. Toss in dried cranberries. Store granola in an airtight container (or freeze).

5. **To Serve:** Spoon about ⅓ cup yogurt into each parfait glass or individual bowl; top with a layer of fruit and sprinkle with granola. Repeat layering once more. Serve immediately.

Norene's Notes

- Variations: In Step 2, add ¼ cup shredded unsweetened coconut to quinoa to boost the fiber. Sunflower seeds and/or mixed nuts are also tasty additions. Play with your food!
- Quinoa and Greek yogurt are packed with protein and will keep you feeling full.

I created this simple roasted squash dish for Shavuot — it's divine. As the sugars in the squash begin to caramelize, the oils in the warm pecans and salty feta cheese become perfect flavor counterpoints. Great for Chanukah as well.

Harvest Squash & Feta

dairy · gluten-free · do not freeze · yields 6-8 servings

Ingredients

1 butternut squash (about 3 lb/1.4 kg), peeled and cut into 1-inch chunks

1½ cups pecan halves

2-3 Tbsp olive oil

3-4 Tbsp pure maple syrup

1 cup crumbled feta cheese

Method

1. Preheat oven to 350°F. Line a rimmed baking sheet with parchment paper.

2. Spread squash and pecans on prepared baking sheet. Drizzle with oil and maple syrup; toss to coat.

3. Bake, uncovered, stirring occasionally, for 35-40 minutes, or until squash is tender-crisp and pecans are a deep amber color.

4. Transfer to a serving platter; sprinkle with feta cheese. Serve immediately.

Norene's Notes

- Microwave Magic: For easier cutting, slash squash in several places with a sharp knife. Place on a paper towel or plate; microwave on high for 5 minutes. Cool slightly. Cut squash in half at the neck, making two pieces: a round ball and an elongated piece. Cut the round bottom part in half; use an ice cream scoop to scoop out and discard seeds and stringy fiber. Peel both halves of the squash and cut it into chunks.

This creamy, flavorful frittata is a great lazy-night dinner that requires minimal brainpower or effort to prepare and is ready in under an hour. But it's also a simple, elegant dish that's perfect for fancier brunches and lunches.

Leek & Goat Cheese Frittata

dairy · passover · gluten-free · freezes well · yields 6 servings

Ingredients

2 Tbsp butter

3 large leeks, white and light green parts only, trimmed and thinly sliced

2 cloves garlic, minced (about 1 tsp)

8 eggs

½ tsp kosher salt

¼ tsp black pepper

½ tsp minced fresh thyme leaves or **pinch** dried thyme

4 oz goat cheese, crumbled

Method

1. Preheat oven to 350°F. Coat the bottom and sides of a 10-inch glass or ceramic quiche dish with nonstick cooking spray.

2. In a large nonstick skillet, heat butter over medium heat until melted and sizzling. Add leeks and garlic; sauté for 6-8 minutes, or until softened. Let cool slightly.

3. In a large bowl, whisk eggs together with salt, pepper, thyme, and goat cheese. Add leek mixture; stir gently to combine.

4. Transfer mixture to prepared baking dish. Bake, uncovered, for 30-35 minutes or until top is set and edges are golden-brown. Serve hot or at room temperature.

Norene's Notes

- As-You-Like-It-Frittata: Add 1 red bell pepper or 1 cup mushrooms, thinly sliced. Instead of thyme, use 1 Tbsp basil. It is also delicious with 1 cup grated Cheddar or Swiss cheese. If desired, top frittata with sliced cherry tomatoes for the last 10 minutes of baking.

- Frittata Muffins: Spray 12 muffin cups with nonstick cooking spray. Prepare frittata mixture as directed. In Step 4, spoon about ⅓ cup mixture into each muffin cup. Bake in a preheated 350°F oven for 20-25 minutes, until set and golden. A perfect grab-and-go breakfast!

- For a lower cholesterol version, substitute 2 egg whites or ¼ cup egg substitute for each egg.

A simple comfort-food dish that's layered with creamy mozzarella, Cheddar, and Parmesan, it's easy to forget there's actually no pasta in this lasagna at all! This is a great dairy-based dish to serve for company, yet is easy enough for weeknight suppers. Perfect for Passover!

Spaghetti Squash Lasagna

dairy · passover · gluten-free · freezes well · yields 6 servings

Ingredients

1 medium spaghetti squash
(about 3 lb/1.4 kg)

2 cups marinara sauce

2 cups chopped
fresh spinach

¼ lb/125 g mozzarella
cheese, sliced

¾ cup grated
Parmesan cheese

2 cups shredded
Cheddar cheese

Method

1. Preheat oven to 350°F. Line a rimmed baking sheet with parchment paper.

2. Cut squash in half lengthwise; discard seeds and pulp. Place squash, cut-side down, on prepared baking sheet. Bake, uncovered, for 35-45 minutes, until tender.

3. Coat the bottom and sides of a 12-inch round glass or ceramic quiche dish with nonstick cooking spray.

4. Use a fork to separate squash strands. Place a layer of squash strands into prepared baking dish. Spoon on 1 cup of marinara sauce. Sprinkle with half the spinach and half the cheeses. Repeat with a second layer, ending with cheeses.

5. Bake, covered, for 30 minutes, until piping hot. Uncover; bake an additional 10 minutes, until golden.

Norene's Notes

- Using your Noodle: For short strands, cut spaghetti squash in half lengthwise. For long strands, cut it into 1-inch rings. Discard seeds and pulp. Place on baking sheet and bake, uncovered, for 35-45 minutes, until tender. Separate squash strands with a fork.

Grain
Side Dishes

Don't let the list of simple ingredients fool you — this magical side dish won't be forgotten! Asparagus, salty olives, and refreshing herbs light up the dish with a surprising combination of flavors. Super yummy, super easy, super for any occasion.

Israeli Couscous Salad
with asparagus & olives

pareve · gluten-free option · do not freeze · yields 6-8 servings

Ingredients

1 bunch asparagus
(about 1 lb/500 g) (snap off
and discard tough ends)

1 Tbsp olive oil

kosher salt

freshly ground black pepper

1½ cups Israeli couscous
(8.8 oz pkg), cooked (see
Norene's Notes, below)

½ cup diced red onion

1 cup kalamata (black)
olives, pitted and halved

Dressing

⅓ cup extra virgin olive oil

2 Tbsp red wine vinegar

2 Tbsp lemon juice
(preferably fresh)

2 tsp Dijon mustard

2 Tbsp honey

1 tsp kosher salt

¼ tsp black pepper

2 cloves garlic, minced
(about 1 tsp)

¼ cup chopped fresh mint
or basil

Method

1. Preheat oven to 400°F. Line a rimmed baking sheet with parchment paper.

2. Spread asparagus in a single layer on baking sheet. Drizzle with oil; sprinkle with salt and pepper. Roast, uncovered, for 8-10 minutes, until tender-crisp. When cool, cut into 1-inch pieces.

3. Meanwhile, cook couscous according to package directions. Fluff with a fork; let cool.

4. In a large serving bowl, combine couscous with asparagus, onion, and olives.

5. **Dressing:** Combine ingredients for dressing in a glass jar; seal tightly and shake well.

6. Add dressing to couscous mixture; mix well. Adjust seasonings to taste. Serve chilled or at room temperature.

Norene's Notes

• Israeli couscous (maftoul) are pearl-shaped grains of pasta. To prepare, you need 1¼ cups lightly salted boiling water or broth for every cup of dried couscous. Simmer, covered, about 10 minutes.

• 1 bunch of asparagus (16-20 spears) weighs about 1 lb/500 g and makes 4 servings. For even cooking, choose asparagus spears that are about the same thickness.

• To make this dish gluten-free, use brown rice couscous, quinoa, or a rice blend; cook according to package directions.

This pretty, simple couscous salad is great for any occasion. Beautiful pomegranate seeds give this dish surprising freshness with a burst of juice in every bite. And since almonds and chickpeas pack some protein, this makes a quick lunch option, too.

Pomegranate Almond Couscous

pareve · gluten-free option · do not freeze · yields 6 servings

Ingredients

1 cup couscous

2 cups boiling water or vegetable broth

1 can (19 oz/540 ml) chickpeas, rinsed and drained

1 cup toasted sliced or slivered almonds

1 cup pomegranate seeds

Dressing

¼ cup extra virgin olive oil

zest and juice of **1** lemon (about 3-4 Tbsp)

2 Tbsp pure maple syrup

1 tsp kosher salt

½ tsp black pepper

½ cup chopped fresh basil

Method

1. Place couscous into a large serving bowl. Add boiling water; cover. Let stand for 10 minutes, until water is absorbed. Fluff with a fork to separate grains. Let cool completely.

2. **Dressing:** Combine ingredients for dressing in a glass jar; seal tightly and shake well.

3. Add chickpeas, almonds, and dressing to couscous; toss to combine. Cover and refrigerate.

4. Add pomegranate seeds shortly before serving. Adjust seasonings to taste. Serve chilled or at room temperature.

Norene's Notes

• No pomegranate seeds? Use dried cranberries, adding them in Step 3.

• Couscous is an excellent item to have on hand in your pantry because it requires no stovetop cooking and minimal preparation.

• Many people think that couscous is a grain, but it is actually tiny grains of pasta made from hard durum wheat. The bran and germ are stripped from the wheat berry; then the endosperm (semolina) is ground, steamed, and dried, forming tiny grains.

This is another oldie but goody. I often find that the older generation knew how to do it best. Both my mom and grandmother would serve this family favorite to us all the time. This Norene Gilletz special is a one-pot dish — what more can you ask for?

One-Pot Mushrooms & Rice

pareve · gluten-free · freezes well · yields 8 servings

Ingredients

2 cups basmati rice

½ lb/250 g assorted mushrooms, trimmed and thinly sliced (about 3 cups)

2 medium onions, halved and thinly sliced

¼ cup soy sauce or tamari

2 Tbsp vegetable oil

2 Tbsp honey

1 tsp kosher salt (or to taste)

½ tsp black pepper

2 tsp garlic powder

1 tsp onion powder

1 tsp dried thyme

3½ cups water or vegetable broth

Method

1. Preheat oven to 350°F. Coat a 9 x 13-inch baking dish with nonstick spray.

2. In a large bowl, combine rice with remaining ingredients; mix well to combine.

3. Transfer to prepared baking dish; cover tightly with foil. Bake for 1 hour, until all liquid has been absorbed.

Norene's Notes

- Variation: In Step 2, add 1 red bell pepper, thinly sliced. If desired, add 1 can (8 oz/ 227 g) sliced water chestnuts, rinsed and drained. Instead of basmati rice, try whole grain brown rice. Always different, always delicious!

My three girls love mango, and this wild rice dish is their latest favorite. The nutty flavor of wild rice is a perfect match for sweet mango and red onion. The dried mango plumps up when marinated in the dressing, adding some softness to the texture of this dish.

Mango Wild Rice

pareve · gluten-free · freezes well · yields 8 servings

Ingredients

4 cups water

1½ cups wild rice, rinsed and drained

1 tsp kosher salt

½ medium red onion, quartered and thinly sliced

12 dried mango slices, thinly sliced into strips

¾ cup dried cranberries

3 Tbsp extra virgin olive oil

⅓ cup orange or mango juice

3 Tbsp honey

½ cup chopped fresh parsley

kosher salt

freshly ground black pepper

Method

1. Bring water to a boil in a medium saucepan over high heat. Add rice and salt; cover. Reduce heat; simmer for about 45 minutes, or until the grains split and burst. Remove from heat; let stand, covered, for 10 minutes. Drain, if necessary. Transfer to a large bowl; let cool.

2. Add onion, dried mangoes, and cranberries. Stir in oil, orange juice, honey, parsley, salt, and pepper. Toss to combine. Adjust seasonings to taste. Serve chilled or at room temperature.

Norene's Notes

- Variation: Since wild rice is fairly expensive, you can use ¾ cup wild rice and ¾ cup whole grain brown rice — their cooking time is about the same.
- No dried mango? Substitute dried apricots.
- Wild rice is gluten-free, fiber-packed, and high in protein and B vitamins. Elegance in health!
- An easy way to cut dried mango is to use kitchen shears.

White basmati rice is a perfect backdrop for lime-green edamame and aromatic dill. This dish works well with any protein and is great when doubled for larger parties.

Dilled Rice
with edamame & dried cranberries

pareve · gluten-free · freezes well · yields 6 servings

Ingredients

1½ cups basmati rice

2 Tbsp olive oil

1 large onion, diced

2 cloves garlic, minced (about 1 tsp)

1 cup frozen shelled edamame beans, thawed and patted dry

1 cup finely chopped fresh dill

½ tsp turmeric

2 tsp kosher salt

½ tsp black pepper

1 cup dried cranberries

Method

1. Cook rice according to package directions.

2. In a large skillet or wok, heat oil over medium-high heat. Add onion, garlic, and edamame beans; sauté for 3-5 minutes, until tender-crisp.

3. Stir in cooked rice, dill, turmeric, salt, pepper, and cranberries. Mix well. Adjust seasonings to taste. Serve hot or at room temperature.

Norene's Notes

- Edamame are tender young soybeans, usually still in their pods. In this recipe, we use them shelled. They are so easy to prepare — why not try them boiled in lightly salted water, steamed, or even sautéed?

- How do you eat edamame beans that are still in the pod? Place the pod into your mouth, then squeeze or bite the edamame — the bean will pop right out. Don't eat the pods, just the beans inside.

- Be careful not to spill turmeric on fabric, as it will quickly dye it bright yellow. Once the stain sets, it can be almost impossible to remove, so it's important to act quickly. Immediately use a clean spoon to remove any excess turmeric, then rinse the fabric with water and dab with a paper towel. Do not rub or scrub, as this will grind in the stain.

A simple rice dish that satisfies on crunch and color, this is an updated version of my mom's go-to staple salad for Shabbat. Mom used to make it with chow mein noodles, but I always like to have a gluten-free option so I switched to Terra Chips. It's a winner!

Terra Chip Rice Salad

pareve · gluten-free · do not freeze · yields 6 servings

Ingredients

1½ cups basmati rice, rinsed and drained

4 scallions, thinly sliced

2 medium carrots, peeled and shredded

1½ cups frozen peas (do not thaw)

2 cups Terra Chips (see Norene's Notes, below)

Dressing

⅓ cup vegetable oil

¼ cup soy sauce or tamari

1 tsp white vinegar

1 tsp sugar

1 tsp curry powder

pinch salt

Method

1. Cook rice according to package directions. Fluff with fork; let cool.

2. Transfer rice to a large serving bowl. Add scallions, carrots, and peas.

3. **Dressing:** Combine dressing ingredients in a glass jar; seal tightly and shake well. Add to salad; mix gently to combine.

4. Shortly before serving, stir in Terra Chips. Serve chilled or at room temperature.

Norene's Notes

- Terra Chips are an exotic mix of root vegetables (e.g., taro, sweet potato) that add crunch to salads and soups. They stay crisp, whereas other vegetable chips might become soggy.
- Variation: This recipe also works well with brown rice, a rice blend, or even quinoa.

This festive dish came together when I was preparing for Succot. I wanted a side dish that offered the elements of fall in a hearty, colorful dish to my guests. The pumpkin seeds add a perfect touch of crunch to set this pretty autumn dish apart from other quinoa salads.

Quinoa & Sweet Potatoes

pareve · passover option · gluten-free · do not freeze · yields 8-10 servings

Ingredients

1 large sweet potato, peeled and diced

1 Tbsp olive oil

kosher salt

freshly ground black pepper

3 cups lightly salted water

1½ cups quinoa, rinsed and drained

1 cup dried cranberries

1½ cups baby spinach, roughly chopped

¾ cup toasted pumpkin seeds, for garnish

Dressing

⅓ cup extra virgin olive oil

⅓ cup red wine vinegar

2 Tbsp pure maple syrup

1 tsp dried basil

1 tsp kosher salt

freshly ground black pepper

Method

1. Preheat oven to 400°F. Line a rimmed baking sheet with parchment paper.

2. Spread diced sweet potato on prepared baking sheet. Drizzle with oil; sprinkle with salt and pepper.

3. Roast, uncovered, for 25-30 minutes, or until tender, stirring occasionally. Let cool.

4. Meanwhile, bring water to a boil in a medium saucepan over high heat. Add quinoa; reduce heat. Simmer, covered, for 15 minutes, or until tender. Remove from heat; let stand for 10 minutes, covered. Fluff quinoa with a fork. Transfer to a large serving bowl; let cool.

5. Add roasted sweet potato, dried cranberries, and spinach to quinoa. Toss to combine.

6. **Dressing:** Combine dressing ingredients in a glass jar; seal tightly and shake well.

7. Add dressing to quinoa mixture; toss to combine. Adjust seasonings to taste. Garnish with pumpkin seeds.

Norene's Notes

- Variations: Substitute 2 cups butternut squash cubes for sweet potato. Instead of dried cranberries, use pomegranate seeds, dried apricots, or raisins. Instead of pumpkin seeds, use sunflower seeds.
- Passover Option: Substitute slivered almonds for pumpkin seeds; use brown sugar or honey instead of maple syrup.

I often build my recipes based on color first and taste second, so unlikely food combinations are the norm in my kitchen. Luckily, the results are usually fantastic, and this simple side is no exception!

Rosy Quinoa

pareve · passover · gluten-free · do not freeze · yields 6-8 servings

Ingredients

1 bunch small yellow or rainbow beets, scrubbed and trimmed (about 4)

3 cups lightly salted water

1½ cups quinoa, rinsed and drained

6 radishes, thinly sliced

1 pink grapefruit, peeled and supremed (cut into membrane-free segments)

½ cup chopped fresh mint or basil

Dressing

⅓ cup extra virgin olive oil

⅓ cup lemon juice

2 Tbsp honey

1 tsp kosher salt

freshly ground black pepper

Method

1. Preheat oven to 350°F. Coat a large piece of heavy-duty foil with nonstick cooking spray. Center beets on foil; wrap tightly, pinching edges together.

2. Bake for 1 hour, or until tender. Carefully open packet and let beets stand until cool enough to handle.

3. Using paper towels, rub off and discard beet skins. Cut beets into half-moons.

4. Meanwhile, bring water to a boil in a medium saucepan over high heat. Add quinoa; reduce heat. Simmer, covered, for 15 minutes, or until tender. Remove from heat; let stand, covered, for 10 minutes. Fluff quinoa with a fork. Transfer to a large serving bowl; let cool.

5. Add beets, radishes, grapefruit, and mint to quinoa; toss to combine.

6. **Dressing:** Combine dressing ingredients in a glass jar; seal tightly and shake well.

7. Shortly before serving, add dressing to quinoa mixture; toss gently to combine. Adjust seasonings to taste. Serve chilled or at room temperature.

Norene's Notes

- Variation: Instead of grapefruit, use 2 medium oranges, supremed (cut into membrane-free segments).
- Short on Time? Replace grapefruit with 1 can (11 oz/312 g) mandarin oranges, drained.

As someone with a gluten-free daughter, I'm obsessed with my Inspiralizer; it turns veggies into spaghetti-like noodles. Of my many faux-noodle dishes, this is the family favorite. Healthy highlights include the protein-packed quinoa, the mango, and the pumpkin seeds.

Zoodles, Quinoa, & More

pareve · passover · gluten-free · do not freeze · yields 6-8 servings

Ingredients

2 cups lightly salted water

1 cup quinoa

2 medium green zucchini, trimmed (do not peel)

2 cups kale, trimmed, cut into bite-sized pieces

1 firm mango, peeled, pitted, and diced

1 red bell pepper, halved, thinly sliced

⅓ cup toasted pumpkin seeds, for garnish

Dressing

⅓ cup extra virgin olive oil

⅓ cup rice vinegar

3 Tbsp soy sauce or tamari

3 Tbsp honey

kosher salt

freshly ground black pepper

2 cloves garlic, minced (about 1 tsp)

Method

1. Bring water to a boil in a medium saucepan over high heat. Add quinoa; reduce heat. Simmer, covered, for 15 minutes, or until tender. Remove from heat; let stand, covered, for 10 minutes. Fluff quinoa with a fork. Transfer to a large serving bowl; let cool.

2. Meanwhile, cut zucchini in half through the width. Set the blade of the spiralizer to the fine noodle setting; spiralize the zucchini, making spaghetti-like noodles. Add to cooled quinoa.

3. Add kale, mango, and red pepper. Cover; refrigerate.

4. **Dressing:** Combine ingredients for dressing in a glass jar; seal tightly and shake well.

5. Shortly before serving, add dressing to salad mixture; toss gently to combine. Adjust seasonings to taste. Garnish with pumpkin seeds. Serve chilled or at room temperature.

Norene's Notes

- A spiralizer is a special spiral vegetable cutter that transforms all sorts of vegetables into noodles. Best of all, veggie noodles are low-carb and gluten-free.
- No spiralizer? Use a vegetable peeler to cut zucchini into long, thin, noodle-like strips or ribbons. As you approach the seeds, rotate the zucchini and start slicing another side. Discard the seeds, as they will prevent the "noodles" from holding together.

Jeffery's late grandfather, Zaidy Vogel, was known for eating anything — except kasha and bows. I thought I'd dare to recreate the recipe in hopes of bringing this classic back to our family table. To my happy surprise, it was a hit! Easy to make, it stays fresh for days.

Veggie Kasha & Bows

pareve · gluten-free option · freezes well · yields 6-8 servings

Ingredients

1½ cups bowtie pasta (gluten-free or regular)

1 cup medium kasha (buckwheat groats)

1 egg, lightly beaten

2 cups hot water or vegetable broth

2 Tbsp grapeseed oil

2 cups sliced mushrooms

2 red bell peppers, quartered and sliced

2 large onions, quartered and sliced

½ cup chopped fresh dill

1½ tsp kosher salt (or to taste)

freshly ground black pepper

Method

1. Cook pasta according to package directions. Drain well; set aside.

2. In a large pot, mix kasha with egg, coating all the grains. Cook over medium heat, stirring often, until kasha is dry and toasted, about 5 minutes.

3. Gradually add water to kasha, being careful to avoid spattering. Stir well. Bring to a boil; reduce heat and simmer, covered, for 10-12 minutes, until water is absorbed. Let stand for 5 minutes. Uncover; fluff with a fork.

4. Meanwhile, in a large skillet or wok, heat oil over medium-high heat. Add mushrooms, peppers, and onions; sauté for 7-8 minutes, until tender-crisp.

5. Combine vegetables, pasta, and dill with kasha; stir to combine. Adjust seasonings to taste. Serve hot.

Norene's Notes

- Surprise! Although the word "wheat" is part of the word buckwheat, it actually contains no wheat! Kasha is gluten-free, packed with protein, iron, calcium, and B-vitamins.
- When you mix kasha with egg and toast it before adding the liquid, the grains develop an earthy, aromatic flavor and will remain separate. If you don't toast the kasha first, it will become mushy.

I put a lot of stock in tradition, especially for the sake of my family. That's why I'm updating some oldies but goodies, like this farfel dish. My husband Jeffery and I grew up eating this, and it still has the same comforting effect on our kids today.

Mushroom & Onion Farfel

pareve · freezes well · yields 4-6 servings

Ingredients

1 pkg farfel
(8 oz/227 oz)
(see Norene's Notes, below)

2 cups sliced mushrooms

2 medium onions, diced

¾ cup chopped fresh parsley

3 Tbsp vegetable oil

1 tsp kosher salt

freshly ground black pepper

1 tsp onion powder

1 tsp garlic powder

2½ cups water or
vegetable broth

Method

1. Preheat oven to 350°F. Coat a 2-quart covered glass baking dish with cooking spray.

2. Combine farfel, mushrooms, onions, parsley, oil, salt, pepper, onion powder, and garlic powder in prepared baking dish. Mix well. Add water; stir to combine.

3. Bake, covered, about 45-50 minutes, until water is absorbed. Serve hot. Adjust seasonings to taste.

Norene's Notes

- Farfel is also known as heimishe farfel or Mama farfel. It is short pasta made from wheat and is not the same as matzo farfel. Heimishe farfel was a popular dish with many immigrant families because it was filling and satisfying — true comfort food!

This cold barley salad is quick to assemble and is great for a buffet table. It can be made ahead of time and doubles easily, which is a bonus when you're super busy. It's fresh and delicious all year around. A winner!

Vegetable Barley Salad

pareve · barley freezes well · yields 6-8 servings

Ingredients

3 cups lightly salted water or vegetable broth

1 cup pearl barley, rinsed and drained

2 medium carrots, peeled and shredded

1 red bell pepper, halved and sliced

2 stalks celery, thinly sliced

2 baby cucumbers, sliced into half moons

2 cups shredded kale

¼ cup chopped fresh basil

1 pint yellow cherry tomatoes, halved

¼ cup extra virgin olive oil

zest and juice of **1** lemon

kosher salt

freshly ground black pepper

Method

1. In a medium saucepan, bring water to a boil. Add barley; simmer, covered, for 40-45 minutes. Transfer barley to a large serving bowl; cool completely. (Can be prepared ahead of time and refrigerated overnight.)

2. Add carrots, bell pepper, celery, cucumbers, kale, basil, and cherry tomatoes to barley.

3. Add oil, lemon zest, and lemon juice to salad; toss to combine. Season generously with salt and pepper. Cover; refrigerate until serving time. Serve chilled.

Norene's Notes

- Pearl barley and pot barley are interchangeable in recipes and their cooking time is about the same. Pot barley still has the endosperm left intact, whereas pearl barley does not.

Farro has a nutty flavor and a chewy texture. This riff on tabbouli brings it to a new level. Grains and greens make a delicious match!

Farro Tabbouli
with cherry tomatoes

pareve · dairy option · do not freeze · yields 6-8 servings

Ingredients

1 cup pearled farro
(see Norene's Notes, below)

pinch salt

4 baby cucumbers,
finely diced (do not peel)

½ red onion, finely diced

2 cups cherry tomatoes,
halved (or multi-colored
tomatoes)

1 cup chopped
fresh parsley leaves

½ **cup** pitted Kalamata
(black) olives, sliced

Dressing

¼ **cup** extra virgin olive oil

¼ **cup** lemon juice
(preferably fresh)

2 cloves garlic, minced
(about 1 tsp)

kosher salt

freshly ground black pepper

½ **tsp** ground cumin

Method

1. In a medium saucepan, toast farro for 2-3 minutes on medium-high heat, until fragrant.

2. Add enough water to fill the pan halfway. Add salt. Bring to a boil. Reduce heat; simmer, partially covered, for 20-25 minutes, until tender. Drain well; let cool. Transfer farro to a large serving bowl.

3. Add cucumbers, onion, cherry tomatoes, parsley, and olives to the bowl. Add dressing ingredients; toss to combine. Cover; refrigerate.

4. Adjust seasonings to taste. Serve chilled.

Norene's Notes

• Farro, which is hulled wheat, refers to three specific wheat species; spelt, emmer, and einkorn. Pearled farro cooks the quickest. If you use regular farro, just increase the cooking time according to package directions.

• A food processor or a mini prep makes quick work of chopping the vegetables and parsley.

• Dairy Variation: In Step 4, sprinkle 1 cup crumbled feta cheese over salad. If desired, add 1 teaspoon za'atar to farro mixture and replace some of the parsley with cilantro or dill.

Lentils are protein-rich, gluten-free, and packed with nutrients. I'm always looking for new ways to use lentils, but sometimes it's best to go back to basics — onions and whole garlic cloves. This dish is a simple, elegant side for any meat, fish, or vegetarian menu.

Caramelized Onion & Garlic Lentils

pareve · gluten-free · do not freeze · yields 6 servings

Ingredients

3 cups water

1 cup dried brown lentils, rinsed and drained

2 Tbsp olive oil

3 large onions, halved and sliced

1 head garlic, peeled and trimmed (about 12-15 cloves) (see Norene's Notes, below)

kosher salt

freshly ground black pepper

½ cup chopped fresh parsley

Method

1. In a medium saucepan, combine water and lentils; bring to a boil. Reduce heat; simmer, covered, for 30-35 minutes, until tender. Drain well.

2. Meanwhile, in a large skillet, heat oil over medium-low heat. Add onions and whole garlic cloves. Sprinkle lightly with salt. Cook slowly for about 30 minutes, until onions have caramelized, stirring occasionally.

3. Gently stir in cooked lentils. Season with salt, pepper, and parsley.

Norene's Notes

- Shortcuts: Instead of using a whole head of garlic, buy packaged individual cloves of peeled garlic. You can also peel garlic easily using a silicone garlic peeler. Just place garlic cloves inside the tube and roll it back and forth. The peels will pop off!

- Variation: Instead of dried brown lentils, substitute black lentils (also known as beluga lentils) — they hold their shape nicely during cooking. Black lentils contain high concentrations of anthocyanins, the same antioxidants found in blueberries. Anthocyanins are believed to improve memory and may reduce the risk of cancer.

Vegetable Side Dishes

When I'm hosting a dinner, I'm always looking for those perfect, flavor-rich dishes that will wow guests without keeping me in the kitchen all night. Loved by everyone, pairs with everything.

Balsamic Asparagus & Tomatoes

pareve · passover · gluten-free · do not freeze · yields 6-8 servings

Ingredients

2 bunches asparagus (about 2 lb/1 kg) (snap off and discard tough ends)

1 pint (about 2 cups) cherry tomatoes

2 Tbsp olive oil

kosher salt

freshly ground black pepper

½ cup balsamic vinegar

2 Tbsp honey

Method

1. Preheat oven to 400°F. Line a rimmed baking sheet with parchment paper.

2. Spread asparagus in a single layer on one side of the baking sheet and spread tomatoes on the other side. Drizzle with oil; sprinkle with salt and pepper.

3. Roast, uncovered, for 10-12 minutes or until asparagus and tomatoes are tender-crisp.

4. Meanwhile, add balsamic vinegar and honey to a small saucepan. Bring to a boil. Reduce heat; simmer, uncovered, until thick, syrupy, and reduced by half, 4-5 minutes. Glaze should coat the back of a spoon.

5. Arrange asparagus spears on an oblong serving platter or individual plates. Spoon the tomatoes over the top. Drizzle with balsamic glaze. Serve hot or at room temperature.

Norene's Notes

- If your cherry tomatoes are on the large side, cut them in half or quarter them.
- Balsamic glaze adds an easy, elegant touch when drizzled over vegetables, fish, poultry, meats, and even salads and berries. Make a quadruple batch, let cool, then store in a jar in your refrigerator. Keeps 1-2 weeks. It'll be gone in a flash!

I can't take full credit for this deliciously simple dish. It was inspired by one of my favorite recipes in Norene's first cookbook (Second Helpings, Please!) — a recipe I grew up on. Easy and healthy, with pops of color, it's a pretty dish for any weeknight get-together.

Peas & Mushrooms

pareve · gluten-free · do not freeze · yields 6 servings

Ingredients

3 Tbsp olive or grapeseed oil

1 large onion,
halved and thinly sliced

1 lb/500 g assorted
mushrooms, sliced
(about 6 cups)

1 bag (16 oz/454 g)
frozen peas
(do not thaw)

1 tsp kosher salt

freshly ground black pepper

Method

1. In a large skillet or wok, heat oil over medium-high heat. Add onion; sauté for 5 minutes, until golden.

2. Add mushrooms; sauté 5-7 minutes longer, until golden.

3. Stir in frozen peas; season with salt and pepper.

4. Cover; simmer for 5-7 minutes, or until peas are heated through. Don't overcook, or peas will lose their bright green color.

5. Adjust seasonings to taste. Serve hot.

Norene's Notes

- Variation: In Step 1, add 1 cup sliced red bell pepper for color. Substitute edamame beans for peas. Add ¼ cup finely chopped fresh mint and/or parsley just before serving.

- Peas have a sweet taste and a starchy texture. They are packed with health-protective phytonutrients, providing anti-oxidant and anti-inflammatory benefits.

- No frozen peas? Use 2 cans (14 oz/400 g each) peas, drained and rinsed. Reduce cooking time in Step 4 to 3-4 minutes.

Candied cauliflower, drizzled with honey and thyme and topped with sliced almonds, is a beautiful dish that will keep your guests coming back for more. I suggest you double the recipe!

Candied Cauliflower
with almonds

pareve · passover · gluten-free · do not freeze · yields 6 servings

Ingredients

1 large cauliflower, trimmed

kosher salt

freshly ground black pepper

1 Tbsp minced
fresh thyme leaves

2 Tbsp olive oil

3 Tbsp honey

½ cup sliced almonds

thyme sprigs, for garnish

Method

1. Preheat oven to 400°F. Line a rimmed baking sheet with parchment paper.

2. Cut cauliflower into 2-inch florets. Transfer to prepared baking sheet.

3. Sprinkle florets with salt, pepper, and thyme. Drizzle with oil and honey. Top with sliced almonds. Rub all over to coat evenly. (Can be prepared up to this point and refrigerated.)

4. Bake, uncovered, for 35-40 minutes, or until cauliflower is golden brown and tender. Serve immediately.

Norene's Notes

- Variation: Use pecan pieces or coarsely chopped cashews instead of almonds. If you have a nut allergy, substitute pumpkin seeds.
- Hot Stuff: Don't worry about the almonds burning. The steam created during cooking prevents that from happening. If your oven is on the hot side, you may prefer to stir in the almonds during the last 15 minutes of baking.
- For tips on buying, cleaning, and storing cauliflower, see Norene's Notes, page 50.

This simple, protein-packed vegetarian dish is a winner! It's easy to double and is perfect for big gatherings. If you have leftovers, toss them into a green salad — nutrition in a bowl!

Cauliflower & Chickpeas

pareve · gluten-free · do not freeze · yields 6 servings

Ingredients

1 large cauliflower, trimmed, cut into florets

1 can (19 oz/540 ml) chickpeas, rinsed and drained

2-3 Tbsp olive oil

1 tsp ground cumin

1 tsp garlic powder

1 tsp sweet paprika

½ tsp kosher salt

freshly ground black pepper

¼ cup chopped fresh parsley, plus more for garnish

juice of **1** lemon, for drizzling

Method

1. Preheat oven to 400°F. Line a rimmed baking sheet with parchment paper.

2. Spread cauliflower florets and chickpeas in a single layer on prepared baking sheet.

3. Drizzle with oil; sprinkle with cumin, garlic powder, paprika, salt, pepper, and parsley. Toss to coat on all sides.

4. Bake, uncovered, for 40-45 minutes, or until tender-crisp.

5. Transfer to a serving dish. Sprinkle with additional parsley; drizzle with lemon juice. Serve hot or at room temperature.

Norene's Notes

- Parsley, with its fresh green flavor and bright color, is much more than a garnish. It adds a fresh, bright flavor to salads, grains, soups, vegetables, main dishes — even sauces and salad dressings.

- Swish parsley in a large bowl of cold water to wash off any sand or dirt; rinse and repeat until clean. Spin dry in a lettuce spinner or wrap in a clean towel to remove excess moisture. Don't discard parsley stems. Add them to homemade soup stocks or stews — they are a great flavor booster.

- For tips on buying, cleaning, and storing cauliflower, see Norene's Notes, page 50.

In Israel, falafel is often topped with French fries (cheeps) and drizzled with tahini sauce. When a tahini craving overwhelmed me, I decided to create this roasted potato substitute. It's delicious, healthy, and has that special Middle Eastern taste.

Oven Baked French Fries
with tahini drizzle

pareve · gluten-free · do not freeze · yields 4-6 servings

Ingredients

6 baking potatoes
(e.g., Idaho, Russet)

2 Tbsp olive oil

2 cloves garlic, minced
(about 1 tsp)

1 tsp ground cumin

kosher salt

freshly ground black pepper

Tahini Sauce

½ cup tahini (sesame paste)

2 Tbsp extra virgin olive oil

¼ cup water

2 Tbsp lemon juice
(preferably fresh)

2 cloves garlic, minced
(about 1 tsp)

kosher salt

¼ cup chopped fresh parsley

Method

1. Preheat oven to 400°F. Line a rimmed baking sheet with parchment paper.

2. Scrub potatoes very well; do not peel. Cut into French fries, about ¼-inch thick.

3. In a large bowl, combine potatoes with oil, garlic, cumin, salt, and pepper. Mix well.

4. Spread potato mixture in a single layer on prepared baking sheet. Roast, uncovered, for 40-45 minutes, or until browned and crispy, stirring once or twice.

5. **Tahini Sauce:** While potatoes are baking, combine ingredients for tahini sauce in a small bowl; stir to combine.

6. Transfer fries to a serving dish. Drizzle with tahini sauce; garnish with parsley. Serve immediately.

Norene's Notes

- Because of its high oil content, refrigerate tahini once it has been open. Stir tahini well before refrigerating. When you take it out of the refrigerator to use, let it stand for a few minutes and stir once again.

- Tahini is terrific as a drizzle over fish or chicken schnitzel. It's also excellent as a dip for crispy raw vegetables or toasted pita. When using it as a dip, drizzle in an additional 2-3 tablespoons water to thin it.

This dish comes together easily and looks so pretty. I make this instead of potato kugel for some Shabbats to lighten up the meal.

Mustard & Garlic Roasted Potatoes

pareve · gluten-free · do not freeze · yields 6-8 servings

Ingredients

2 lb/1 kg potatoes (mix of red and white) cut into wedges (do not peel)

2 large onions, trimmed and cut into large chunks

⅓ cup whole grain Dijon mustard

2 Tbsp extra virgin olive oil

2 Tbsp lemon juice (preferably fresh)

4 cloves garlic, minced (about 2 tsp)

1 Tbsp dried oregano

1 tsp kosher salt

freshly ground black pepper

¼ cup thinly sliced chives, for garnish

Method

1. Preheat oven to 400°F. Line a rimmed baking sheet with parchment paper.

2. In a large bowl, toss potatoes well with onions, mustard, oil, lemon juice, garlic, oregano, salt, and pepper. Spread evenly on prepared baking sheet.

3. Bake, uncovered, for 45 minutes, or until tender-crisp, stirring occasionally. Garnish with chives. Serve hot or at room temperature.

Norene's Notes

- Variation: You can use fingerling potatoes as an alternative; they are a great choice for roasting. Use red baby potatoes (not peeled) as well; they will add beautiful color to the dish.

Simple, savory, and sweet, this recipe is a perfect potato option for any dinner menu. Speckled with rich, toasted sesame seeds, this simple, elegant dish will impress your guests while only taking minutes to prep. Luckily, this recipe multiplies easily for a crowd.

Sesame Sweet Potatoes

pareve · gluten-free · freezes well · yields 4 servings

Ingredients

4 medium sweet potatoes (about 2 lb/1 kg), peeled, cut into 1-inch chunks

1 tsp kosher salt

¼ tsp black pepper

1 tsp garlic powder

1 tsp onion powder

2-3 Tbsp olive oil

3 Tbsp pure maple syrup

¼ cup sesame seeds

Method

1. Preheat oven to 400°F. Line a rimmed baking sheet with parchment paper.

2. In a large bowl, sprinkle sweet potatoes with salt, pepper, garlic powder, and onion powder. Drizzle with olive oil and maple syrup. Mix well.

3. Spread in a single layer on prepared baking sheet.

4. Bake, uncovered, for 35-40 minutes, stirring occasionally.

5. Sprinkle with sesame seeds; bake 10-15 minutes, until tender-crisp and golden. Serve hot.

Norene's Notes

- Buying Guideline: 1 lb/500 g sweet potatoes are equal to two medium sweet potatoes.
- Large, starchy, and sweet tasting, the sweet potato is only distantly related to the potato and does not belong to the nightshade family — happy news for those of you who suffer from arthritis. (People with arthritis often avoid nightshade vegetables, such as potatoes, eggplants, and peppers.)

Passover was a creative time this past year, because I wanted to serve something new! Craving something sweet and crunchy, I whipped up this scrumptious dish. More than just a Pesach treat, this simple roasted vegetable dish is an easy one to make year 'round.

Roasted Vegetables
with terra chips

pareve • passover • gluten-free • veggies freeze well • yields 6 servings

Ingredients

4 medium beets
(about 1 lb/500 g),
peeled, cut into chunks

2 medium sweet potatoes
(about 1 lb/500 g),
peeled, cut into chunks

3 cups butternut squash,
cut into chunks

3 Tbsp olive oil

¼ cup honey

3 cloves garlic, minced
(about 1½ tsp)

2 tsp minced fresh rosemary
or thyme

kosher salt

freshly ground black pepper

1 tsp ground cinnamon

1½ cups coarsely crushed
terra chips

Method

1. Preheat oven to 400°F. Line a rimmed baking sheet with parchment paper.

2. In a large bowl, combine beets, sweet potatoes, and squash. Add oil, honey, garlic, rosemary, salt, pepper, and cinnamon. Mix well.

3. Spread in a single layer on prepared baking sheet.

4. Bake, uncovered, for 45-50 minutes, or until tender crisp, stirring occasionally.

5. Transfer to a serving bowl; sprinkle with terra chips. Serve hot or at room temperature.

Norene's Notes

• Variation: Instead of terra chips, use potato chips or coarsely crushed gluten-free crackers.

• Peeling Beets: Use disposable gloves, as beets tend to stain your hands. Alternatively, after roasting whole beets, rub off the skins with a paper towel.

• To prevent stains, cover your cutting board with paper towels before cutting beets. To clean a beet-stained cutting board, make a coarse paste of salt, water, and baking soda; scrub it on the stain with a brush.

Big on elegance, this maple syrup-infused dish is as beautiful as it is delicious. Parsnips add another dimension of texture and color that really make this dish pop.

Roasted Carrots, Parsnips & Sweet Potatoes

pareve · gluten-free · freezes well · yields 6 servings

Ingredients

2 bunches carrots, trimmed, peeled, and sliced lengthwise

6 large parsnips, trimmed, peeled, and sliced lengthwise

2 large sweet potatoes, peeled and sliced lengthwise

¼ cup olive oil

3 Tbsp pure maple syrup

3 Tbsp balsamic vinegar

3 cloves garlic, minced (about 1½ tsp)

2 tsp minced fresh thyme

1 tsp minced fresh rosemary

1½ tsp kosher salt

freshly ground black pepper

thyme and rosemary sprigs, for garnish

Method

1. Preheat oven to 400°F. Line a rimmed baking sheet with parchment paper.

2. Combine carrots, parsnips, and sweet potatoes in a large bowl. Add oil, maple syrup, vinegar, garlic, thyme, rosemary, salt, and pepper. Mix well to coat veggies.

3. Spread in a single layer on prepared baking sheet.

4. Roast, uncovered, for 35-45 minutes, or until fork tender and glazed.

5. Transfer to a platter; garnish with thyme and rosemary sprigs. Serve hot.

Norene's Notes

- Larger carrots often have a woody center, while smaller carrots are sweeter and more tender. It's best to purchase carrots with their tops still attached, because they are fresher and more flavorful.

- Carrots are packed with beta-carotene and also contain lutein and zeaxanthin, which are essential for eye health. Carrots help promote good vision, especially night vision.

Why do we only use granola in dishes served before noon? Crunchy, wholesome, and rustic, the delicious oaty mixture makes a sophisticated and surprising topping for a sweet potato gratin. This is an easy, impress-your-guests dish for any occasion.

Sweet Potato Gratin
with maple granola topping

pareve · gluten-free option · freezes well · yields 8 servings

Ingredients

Granola Topping

1½ cups rolled oats (gluten-free or regular)

2 Tbsp brown sugar

1½ tsp ground cinnamon

2 Tbsp grapeseed oil

3 Tbsp pure maple syrup

pinch kosher salt

¾ cup assorted chopped nuts (e.g., almonds, walnuts, pecans)

½ cup assorted seeds (e.g., pumpkin, sunflower)

Sweet Potatoes

4 large sweet potatoes (about 2 lb/1 kg), peeled, cut into chunks

kosher salt

freshly ground black pepper

1 Tbsp extra virgin olive oil

2 Tbsp pure maple syrup

Method

1. Preheat oven to 325°F. Line a rimmed baking sheet with parchment paper.

2. **Granola:** In a medium bowl, combine oats with brown sugar, cinnamon, oil, maple syrup, salt, nuts, and seeds. Mix well.

3. Spread granola mixture evenly on prepared baking sheet. Bake for 30-35 minutes, or until golden, stirring occasionally.

4. **Sweet potatoes:** Meanwhile, bring a large pot of salted water to a boil. Add sweet potatoes; reduce heat. Simmer for 20-25 minutes, until tender. Drain well.

5. Return sweet potatoes to pot. Add salt, pepper, oil, and maple syrup. Mash until smooth, adding water if necessary to make a creamy texture.

6. Remove granola from oven; allow to cool slightly. Coat a 9 x 13-inch baking dish with nonstick spray. Spread sweet potatoes evenly in baking dish; top with granola.

7. Bake, uncovered, for about 25 minutes, until heated through. Serve hot.

Norene's Notes

- Variation: Substitute butternut squash for sweet potatoes (or use a combination of mashed butternut squash and sweet potatoes).
- Rushed for time? Use store-bought granola as a topping. Use frozen or prepackaged sweet potato and/or butternut squash cubes.

Tradition! You really can't go wrong with classic potato latkes. I've added four unique toppings to serve alongside, each with its own flavor. Make a different topping every night and delight your guests!

Classic Potato Latkes
with assorted toppings

pareve · passover · gluten-free · latkes freeze well · yields about 2 dozen

Ingredients

6 large potatoes (preferably Idaho/russet), peeled and cut into chunks

1 large onion, cut into chunks

2 eggs

¼ cup potato starch

1 tsp baking powder

1 tsp kosher salt

¼ tsp black pepper

grapeseed oil, for frying

Method

1. Preheat oven to 250°F. Line a rimmed baking sheet with parchment paper.

2. In a food processor fitted with the shredding disk, shred potatoes and onion, using medium pressure. Transfer vegetables to a large colander set in the sink or over a large bowl; press firmly to drain excess liquid.

3. Place drained veggies into a large bowl. Add eggs, potato starch, baking powder, salt, and pepper. Mix well.

4. In a large skillet, heat oil over medium-high heat. Working in batches, drop large spoonfuls of batter into hot oil to form pancakes, flattening them slightly with the back of the spoon. Do not crowd the skillet. Fry for 3-4 minutes per side, or until crisp and golden.

5. Drain well on paper towels. Transfer to prepared baking sheet; place into oven to keep warm.

Norene's Notes

- Freeze with Ease: Arrange latkes in a single layer on a baking sheet; freeze until firm. Transfer to resealable plastic bags, press out all air, and freeze. To reheat, place frozen latkes onto a large baking sheet. Bake, uncovered, at 400°F for 12-15 minutes, until hot and crisp.
- Note: Do not freeze toppings!

Sour Cream Topping 2 Ways

dairy • pareve option • passover • gluten-free • yields 4-6 servings

Ingredients

1 cup sour cream (regular or low fat) or Tofutti sour cream

1 Tbsp lemon juice

¼ cup chopped fresh parsley or dill

freshly ground black pepper

½ cup pomegranate seeds, or **¼ lb/125 g** fresh smoked salmon, thinly sliced

Method

1. In a medium bowl, combine sour cream with lemon juice, parsley (if using pomegranate seeds) or dill (if using smoked salmon), and pepper; mix well.

2. Top latkes; add pomegranate seeds (if using parsley) or smoked salmon (if using dill).

Deli Topping

meat • passover • gluten-free • yields 4-6 servings

Ingredients

1 Tbsp Dijon mustard

2 tsp honey

3 Israeli pickles, diced

½ lb/250 g deli meat, diced

Method

1. Add topping ingredients to medium bowl; mix to combine. Use as a topping for latkes.

Avocado Topping

pareve • passover • gluten-free • yields 4-6 servings

Ingredients

1 ripe avocado, peeled, pitted, and diced

¼ cup minced red onion

1 tomato, diced

1 Tbsp lime juice, preferably fresh

1 tsp kosher salt

freshly ground black pepper

Method

1. Add topping ingredients to medium bowl; mix to combine. Place plastic wrap directly onto mixture to prevent darkening.

2. Right before serving, top latkes with avocado mixture.

Just perfectly cooked mushrooms in a sweet yet savory sauce: This simple dish puts mushrooms on a pedestal to showcase their meaty flavor and texture. Side bonus: As a single-item dish, you'll save yourself the hassle of chopping a variety of veggies!

Roasted Sweet & Savory Mushrooms

pareve · gluten-free · do not freeze · yields 4-6 servings

Ingredients

1½ lb/750 g
(about 9 cups) assorted
mushrooms, sliced

3 Tbsp olive oil

3 Tbsp soy sauce or tamari

3 Tbsp honey

2 tsp minced fresh rosemary
or **¼ tsp** dried

kosher salt

freshly ground black pepper

rosemary sprigs, for garnish,
optional

Method

1. Preheat oven to 400°F. Line a rimmed baking sheet with parchment paper.

2. In a large bowl, combine mushrooms with oil, soy sauce, and honey. Sprinkle with rosemary, salt, and pepper. Toss to combine.

3. Spread mushrooms on prepared baking sheet. Roast, uncovered, for 25-30 minutes, or until nicely browned, stirring occasionally.

4. Transfer to a serving platter. Garnish with fresh rosemary sprigs, if desired.

Norene's Notes

- Rosemary sprigs have a strong, somewhat woodsy aroma. Did you know that rosemary is believed to help improve memory?
- To mince rosemary, strip the leaves from the woody stem and chop them finely, as they are quite tough. An easy way to remove the leaves is to pinch the stem near the top with the fingers of one hand, then run the fingers of your other hand down the stem from top to bottom.
- Buying Guide: 1 lb/500 g of mushrooms is about 6 cups.

This crispy, crunchy squash recipe works well for both casual and holiday occasions. The surprising combination of dill and maple syrup in the topping really makes this dish sing.

Panko-Topped Squash Crescents

pareve · gluten-free option · do not freeze · yields 8 servings

Ingredients

1 buttercup or acorn squash
(about 2 lb/1 kg)
(do not peel)

1½ cups panko crumbs
(gluten-free or regular)

4 cloves garlic, minced
(about 2 tsp)

¼ **cup** chopped fresh parsley

¼ **cup** chopped fresh dill

⅓ **cup** pure maple syrup

¼ **cup** olive oil

kosher salt

freshly ground black pepper

Method

1. Preheat oven to 375°F. Line two rimmed baking sheets with parchment paper.

2. Microwave squash on high power for 5 minutes. (No need to pierce it first, as microwaving only softens the squash slightly for easier cutting.)

3. Cut squash in half crosswise; remove and discard seeds and fibers. Cut into crescents, about ½-inch thick. Arrange slices in a single layer on prepared baking sheets.

4. In a large bowl, combine panko, garlic, parsley, dill, maple syrup, oil, salt, and pepper. Mix well.

5. Spoon a layer of crumb mixture onto each squash crescent. Bake, uncovered, for 35-40 minutes or until squash is tender crisp. Serve hot.

Norene's Notes

- Variation: Kick it up a notch by adding ½ teaspoon each of curry powder, turmeric, and cayenne pepper to the panko mix.
- No microwave? For easier cutting, in Step 2, bake squash at 375°F for 15 minutes.
- Do Ahead: Slice the squash a day in advance and refrigerate it in a resealable plastic bag. Ready when you are!

Faux "fried rice" is the latest trend. Cauliflower is processed in a food processor until it reaches the consistency of rice, becoming the base for this yummy side dish.

Cauliflower Rainbow "Rice"

pareve · passover option · gluten-free · do not freeze · yields 4-6 servings

Ingredients

1 medium head cauliflower, broken into florets

2-3 Tbsp grapeseed oil

2 medium onions, diced

4 cloves garlic, minced (about 2 tsp)

2 medium carrots, diced (about 1 cup)

½ red bell pepper, diced

½ yellow bell pepper, diced

1 cup small broccoli florets

1 cup frozen peas or shelled edamame beans (do not thaw)

⅓ cup soy sauce or tamari

1 Tbsp honey

2 Tbsp toasted sesame oil (optional)

kosher salt

freshly ground black pepper

2 scallions, thinly sliced, for garnish

Method

1. Working in batches, process cauliflower in the bowl of a food processor fitted with the "S" blade, using quick on/off pulses, until it resembles grains of rice. Do not over-process. (See Norene's Notes, below.)

2. In a wok or large skillet, heat oil over medium-high heat. Add onions and garlic; stir-fry for 5 minutes, until golden. Add carrots, peppers, and broccoli; cook until tender-crisp, about 5 minutes longer.

3. Stir in peas and cauliflower "rice." Mix well. Cook for 3-4 minutes, until heated through.

4. Drizzle in soy sauce, honey, sesame oil, salt, and pepper; mix well. Adjust seasonings to taste. Transfer to a large platter; garnish with scallions.

Norene's Notes

- Time-Saving Tip: Transfer processed cauliflower to a large platter. Then process the onions, garlic, carrots, and peppers in small batches in the food processor using quick on/off pulses, until coarsely chopped. Do not over-process.
- Passover Version: Omit peas, soy sauce, and sesame oil. Sauté 1-2 cups sliced mushrooms in Step 2 along with onions and garlic.

Cookies & Treats

These chow mein mounds were one of my favorite treats as a kid (and may help to explain my early and ongoing chocolate fixation). Smothered in chocolate, the crunchy noodles have a creepy-crawly look that adds some fun to the dessert table. Great to make with kids!

Chocolate Mounds

pareve · passover · gluten-free option · freezes well · yields about 2 dozen

Ingredients

1 bar (14 oz/400 g) semisweet chocolate, broken into chunks

3 cups chow mein noodles (gluten-free, regular, or Passover)

2 cups mini marshmallows

Method

1. Line a rimmed baking sheet with parchment paper.

2. Pour about 1 inch of water into a saucepan. Bring to a boil; reduce heat to a simmer.

3. Place chocolate into a large, dry, heatproof bowl wider than the saucepan. Place bowl over simmering water. Melt chocolate, stirring often. Cool for 5 minutes.

4. Stir in noodles and marshmallows. Using a large cookie scoop, form mixture into golf-ball-size mounds. Arrange mounds in a single layer on prepared baking sheet.

5. Refrigerate for 45 minutes, or until set. Store in an airtight container in the refrigerator or freezer.

Norene's Notes

- Make sure that no water gets into the chocolate in Step 3. If water mixes with the chocolate, the chocolate will not melt properly.

- It's important to cool the chocolate before adding the marshmallows in Step 3 or they will melt and disappear.

- Variations: Add colored mini marshmallows instead of white ones. Add 1 cup shredded coconut to melted chocolate at the beginning of Step 4.

I thought I couldn't top my chocolate chip cookies from my first book, but these are so amazing! They have a rich, fudgy brownie taste — only in cookie form. They're just as delicious hot from the oven as they are straight out of the freezer (that's how I like to eat them).

The Ultimate Chewy Chocolate Brownie Cookie

pareve • gluten-free option • freezes well • yields 15 cookies

Ingredients

2 eggs

½ cup vegetable oil

1 cup brown sugar, lightly packed

¼ cup granulated sugar

1 tsp pure vanilla extract

½ cup chocolate chips, melted and slightly cooled

1 cup flour (or gluten-free flour with xanthum gum)

½ cup unsweetened cocoa powder

½ tsp baking soda

pinch salt

1 cup chocolate chunks

Method

1. In a large bowl, combine eggs, oil, sugars, and vanilla. Using a wooden spoon, mix until well blended, 1-2 minutes. Stir in melted chocolate chips.

2. Add flour, cocoa, baking soda, and salt; mix just until combined. Stir in chocolate chunks.

3. Cover; refrigerate for 30 minutes.

4. Preheat oven to 350°F. Line two baking sheets with parchment paper.

5. Using a large cookie scoop, drop golf-ball-size mounds of dough 2 inches apart onto prepared baking sheets.

6. Bake for 11-13 minutes, until set. Let cool on baking sheets. Store at room temperature in an airtight container.

Norene's Notes

- When baking two pans of cookies at the same time, place oven racks so they divide the oven evenly into thirds.
- No cookie scoop? Use a ¼-cup measuring cup and cut each mound in half.
- Freeze with Ease: Scoop out balls of dough; place them on a parchment-lined baking sheet. Freeze for 1-2 hours. Transfer frozen cookies to a resealable freezer bag. Bake them straight from the freezer, increasing baking time by 1-2 minutes.

Dense and chewy, these yummy granola cookies are a family favorite. This is a great way to add some healthy fiber to your day. Cookies for breakfast, anyone?

Chocolate Chip Granola Cookies

pareve · gluten-free option · freezes well · yields about 30 cookies

Ingredients

2 eggs

½ cup vegetable oil

1 cup brown sugar, firmly packed

¼ cup granulated sugar

2 tsp pure vanilla extract

1½ cups flour (or gluten-free flour with xanthum gum)

½ tsp baking soda

pinch salt

1 tsp ground cinnamon

3½ cups granola (store-bought or home-made; see page 256) (regular or gluten-free)

1½ cups chocolate chips

Method

1. In a large bowl, combine eggs, oil, sugars, and vanilla. Using a wooden spoon, mix until well blended, 1-2 minutes.

2. Add flour, baking soda, salt, and cinnamon; mix just until combined. Stir in granola and chocolate chips.

3. Cover; refrigerate for 45 minutes.

4. Preheat oven to 350°F. Line two rimmed baking sheets with parchment paper.

5. Using a large cookie scoop, drop golf-ball-size mounds of dough 2 inches apart onto prepared baking sheets.

6. Bake for 13-15 minutes, until golden. Let cool on baking sheet. Store at room temperature in an airtight container.

Norene's Notes

- Variation: Instead of chocolate chips, use pareve or dairy white chocolate chips. Dried cranberries, blueberries, or raisins would also work well.
- Switch-up! When baking two pans of cookies at the same time, reverse them from front to back and from top to bottom halfway through.
- Quick Tip: Mark the front edge of the parchment paper to indicate which pan starts on the top and which starts on the bottom. This helps keep track of which edge goes where when you reverse the pans.

I can't get enough of the coconut craze! Coconut adds a sweet, nutty flavor and flaky texture to this no-fail biscotti recipe. Combine that with chocolate and crunch, and you have a perfect post-dinner indulgence. Delicious served with tea or coffee.

Chocolate Coconut Biscotti

pareve · gluten-free option · freezes well · yields 2-3 dozen

Ingredients

3 eggs

½ cup vegetable or coconut oil

2 tsp pure vanilla extract

1¼ cups sugar or coconut sugar

2 cups flour (or gluten-free flour with xanthum gum)

¾ cup unsweetened cocoa powder

1 tsp baking soda

pinch salt

1½ cups shaved or flaked coconut

1½ cups chocolate chips (regular or mini)

Method

1. Preheat oven to 350°F. Line a large rimmed baking sheet with parchment paper.

2. In a large mixing bowl, whisk together eggs, oil, vanilla, and sugar until well blended. Stir in flour, cocoa, baking soda, and salt, making a sticky, thick batter. Gently stir in coconut and chocolate chips.

3. Transfer dough to prepared baking sheet and shape into two long, narrow logs (about 1½-inches wide). Wet your hands for easier handling.

4. Bake for 30 minutes, or until firm. Remove from oven; let cool for 10-15 minutes.

5. Reduce oven temperature to 300°F. Using a serrated or electric knife, cut logs into slices about ¾-inch thick. Place slices cut side up in a single layer on baking sheet. For softer biscotti, bake cut slices for 20 minutes. For dry, crisp biscotti, bake for 30 minutes. Let cool completely.

Norene's Notes

- I like to use aluminum half-sheet pans for baking biscotti (and other cookies) because they conduct the heat evenly and prevent burning.
- An electric knife slices biscotti beautifully. Just remember to slice them while they are still warm.

Chocolate bark is tan edible canvas for being creative with color, pattern, and texture. Try these options, or apply the preparation method to create your own.

Chocolate Bark

all variations freeze well · yields 8 servings each

Seeded Chocolate Bark

pareve · gluten-free

Ingredients

1 bar (14 oz/400 g) semisweet chocolate, broken into chunks

½ cup hemp or pumpkin seeds

½ cup chia seeds

½ cup white quinoa (not cooked)

coarse sea salt, for sprinkling

Method

1. Line a rimmed baking sheet with parchment paper.

2. Pour about 1 inch of water into a saucepan. Bring to a boil; reduce heat to a simmer.

3. Place chocolate into a large, dry, heatproof bowl wider than the saucepan. Place bowl over simmering water. Melt chocolate, stirring often. Cool slightly.

4. Stir in hemp seeds, chia seeds, and quinoa. Pour mixture onto prepared pan; spread evenly. Sprinkle lightly with sea salt.

5. Refrigerate for 45 minutes, until chocolate is set.

6. Break into small, irregular pieces. Store in an airtight container in the refrigerator or freezer.

White Chocolate Bark

dairy · pareve option · passover · gluten-free

Ingredients

4 bars (3.5 oz/100 g each) white milk chocolate, broken into chunks

1½ cups shelled pistachios

1½ cups dried cranberries

Method

1. Line a rimmed baking sheet with parchment paper.

2. Pour about 1 inch of water into a saucepan. Bring to a boil; reduce heat to a simmer.

3. Place chocolate into a large, dry, heatproof bowl wider than the saucepan. Place bowl over simmering water. Melt chocolate, stirring often. Cool slightly.

4. Stir half the pistachios and cranberries into melted chocolate. Pour mixture onto prepared pan; spread evenly. Sprinkle with remaining pistachios and cranberries, pressing them gently into chocolate.

5. Refrigerate for 45 minutes, until chocolate is set.

6. Break into small, irregular pieces. Store in an airtight container in the refrigerator or freezer.

Norene's Notes

• Semisweet and bittersweet chocolate are interchangeable in the chocolate bark recipes.

Norene's Notes

• Pareve Option: Use 2 (8.8 oz/250 g) pkgs pareve white chocolate chips.

Cookie Chocolate Bark

pareve • gluten-free option

Ingredients

1 bar (14 oz/400 g) semisweet chocolate, broken into chunks

2½ cups coarsely crushed cookies, such as chocolate chip or sandwich cookies (regular or gluten-free)

Method

1. Line a rimmed baking sheet with parchment paper.

2. Pour about 1 inch of water into a saucepan. Bring to a boil; reduce heat to a simmer.

3. Place chocolate into a large, dry, heatproof bowl wider than the saucepan. Place bowl over simmering water. Melt chocolate, stirring often. Cool slightly.

4. Stir half the crushed cookies into melted chocolate. Pour mixture onto prepared pan; spread evenly. Sprinkle with remaining crushed cookies; press gently into chocolate.

5. Refrigerate for 45 minutes, until chocolate is set.

6. Break into small, irregular pieces. Store in an airtight container in the refrigerator or freezer.

Norene's Notes

• Don't worry if your chocolate bar is not the exact weight — just increase the add-ins accordingly.

Nutella Chocolate Bark

dairy • pareve option • gluten-free

Ingredients

1 bar (14 oz/400 g) semisweet chocolate, broken into chunks

1 cup Nutella chocolate hazelnut spread

2½ cups crushed salted mixed nuts, such as hazelnuts, almonds, pecans, cashews

Method

1. Line a rimmed baking sheet with parchment paper.

2. Pour about 1 inch of water into a saucepan. Bring to a boil; reduce heat to a simmer.

3. Place chocolate into a large, dry, heatproof bowl wider than the saucepan. Place bowl over simmering water. Melt chocolate, stirring often. Cool slightly.

4. Stir Nutella and half the nut mixture into melted chocolate. Pour mixture onto prepared pan; spread evenly. Sprinkle with remaining nuts; press gently into chocolate.

5. Refrigerate for 45 minutes, until chocolate is set.

6. Break into small, irregular pieces. Store in an airtight container in the refrigerator or freezer.

Norene's Notes

• Pareve Option: Use Israeli chocolate-flavored spread instead of Nutella, which is dairy.

A cookie, a blondie, and a popcorn ball, all rolled into one. This is a terrific treat to serve to dessert lovers, young and old. Easy to make, easy to freeze, and, in my experience, a prize-winning dish at bake sales!

Chocolate Chip Popcorn Blondies

pareve · gluten-free option · omit popcorn if freezing · yields 3 dozen

Ingredients

Base

¾ cup vegetable oil

1¼ cups brown sugar, lightly packed

2 eggs

1 tsp pure vanilla extract

2 cups flour (or gluten-free flour with xanthum gum)

1 tsp baking soda

pinch salt

1 cup chocolate chips

Topping

2 cups chocolate chips

4 cups popped lightly salted popcorn

Method

1. Preheat oven to 350°F. Coat a 9 x 13-inch baking pan with nonstick cooking spray.

2. **Base:** In a large mixing bowl, combine oil, brown sugar, eggs, and vanilla. Mix until well blended. Add flour, baking soda, and salt; stir to combine. Stir in chocolate chips.

3. Spread mixture evenly in prepared pan. Bake for 20-25 minutes, until golden. (It will be slightly underdone, but that's okay.)

4. **Topping:** Remove pan from oven and sprinkle with chocolate chips. Return to oven; bake for an additional 5 minutes, until chocolate chips have melted.

5. Remove pan from oven. Spread chocolate across cake. Top evenly with popcorn; pat down gently but firmly, so it sticks to the melted chocolate.

6. Let cool completely. Cut into bars. Store in an airtight container at room temperature.

Norene's Notes

- Variation: Use 3 cups caramel popcorn instead of plain.
- For added elegance, drizzle popcorn with an additional ½ cup melted chocolate chips at the end of Step 5.
- These blondies are also good on their own. If preferred, omit popcorn.

With a little creativity, you can indulge in both cookies and brownies at the same time! This no-compromise dessert is the peanut butter cup of the cookie world. Rich, chocolaty brownies wrap around peanut butter cookie centers — it's the perfect bite.

Peanut Butter Cookie Brownies

pareve · gluten-free option · freezes well · yields 12 bars

Ingredients

Brownie Batter

½ cup vegetable oil

1 cup sugar

2 eggs

1 tsp pure vanilla extract

½ cup flour (or gluten-free flour with xanthum gum)

⅓ cup unsweetened cocoa powder

pinch salt

¼ tsp baking powder

Cookie Batter

½ cup creamy peanut butter or Wowbutter soy spread

6 Tbsp brown sugar

1 egg yolk

Method

1. Preheat oven to 350°F. Spray a 7 x 11-inch baking pan with nonstick cooking spray.

2. **Brownie Batter:** In a large bowl, combine oil, sugar, eggs, and vanilla; mix with a wooden spoon until well blended. Add flour, cocoa, salt, and baking powder; stir just until blended. Spread evenly in prepared baking pan.

3. **Cookie Batter:** In a medium bowl, combine peanut butter, brown sugar, and egg yolk; mix until well blended.

4. Drop rounded teaspoons of cookie batter onto the brownie base, forming 12 cookies.

5. Bake, uncovered, for 28-30 minutes, or until a toothpick inserted into the center comes out almost clean. When completely cooled, cut into bars. Store in an airtight container.

Norene's Notes

- Don't overbake brownies. A wooden toothpick inserted into the center should come out with a few moist crumbs clinging to it.

An updated take on a childhood favorite, these nosh-worthy cereal bites are completely irresistible, even for adults. They're simple enough for last-minute bake sales, yet sophisticated enough for dinner parties.

Chocolate Peanut Butter Bites

pareve · gluten-free · freezes well · yields 8-10 servings

Ingredients

1 bag (10 oz/300 g) chocolate chips

½ cup peanut butter, almond butter, or Wowbutter soy spread

8 cups Chex cereal (regular or gluten-free)

1½ cups confectioners' sugar

Method

1. In a large, heavy-bottomed pot, heat chocolate chips and peanut butter together over low heat until melted and smooth. Stir often.

2. Add cereal; mix gently until cereal is completely coated, being careful not to break the cereal. Cool for 2-3 minutes.

3. Place confectioners' sugar into a large resealable bag. Carefully spoon chocolate-coated cereal into the bag; seal tightly. Shake well, coating cereal with confectioners' sugar. The chocolate-coated cereal will stick together to form chunks.

4. Store in the refrigerator or freezer. Serve in martini or wine glasses.

Norene's Notes

- Variation: Use white chocolate chips instead of regular chocolate chips. For a fun presentation, add 1 cup of crushed candy canes to the cereal mixture in Step 2.

Who doesn't love orange and chocolate? This simple muffin recipe brings these lush flavors together into an irresistible, on-the-go snack. Orange juice keeps these muffins moist, and orange zest gives them that bright, citrus flavor. A great addition for every lunch bag in your family!

Orange-Infused Chocolate Chip Muffins

pareve · gluten-free option · freezes well · yield about 18 muffins

Ingredients

3 eggs

1 cup vegetable oil

1 cup sugar

1½ Tbsp fresh orange zest

6 Tbsp orange juice (preferably fresh)

1½ cups flour (or gluten-free flour with xanthan gum)

1½ tsp baking powder

½ tsp baking soda

pinch salt

1½ cups chocolate chips

Method

1. Preheat oven to 350°F. Line muffin pans with paper liners.

2. In a large bowl, combine eggs, oil, and sugar. Whisk together until light, about 2 minutes. Stir in orange zest and juice.

3. Add flour, baking powder, baking soda, and salt; whisk together just until combined. Stir in chocolate chips.

4. Scoop batter into paper-lined muffin pans, filling them ¾-full. Bake for 20-25 minutes, until golden.

Norene's Notes

- Measure Up: Use metal or hard plastic measuring cups for dry ingredients; use clear glass measuring cups with a spout to measure liquids. Use the same measuring spoons for dry and liquid measures.

- How to Measure Flour: Stir flour to loosen it. Dip a measuring cup deep into the container. Scoop flour into cup, making sure there are no air pockets. Don't pack flour. Level off with the flat side of a knife or metal spatula so that flour is level with the cup rim. Never measure flour in a glass measuring cup and never "knuck" the cup to level the flour!

From bake sales to birthdays, rice crispy squares are a classic North American treat. I've amplified this simple and slightly guilty pleasure by giving it a chocolate bar twist. It comes together in minutes — all you have to do is let the chocolate firm up.

Crispy Peanut Butter Bars

pareve · gluten-free option · freezes well · yields about 2 dozen

Ingredients

¾ cup honey

1 cup peanut butter or Wowbutter soy spread

1 tsp pure vanilla extract

1 cup coarsely chopped peanuts (optional)

4 cups crisp rice cereal (gluten-free or regular)

1 cup chocolate chips, melted

Method

1. Line a 9 x 9-inch baking pan with parchment paper.

2. Combine honey and peanut butter in a large saucepan over medium-low heat; stir until melted.

3. Add vanilla and peanuts; mix to combine.

4. Stir in cereal; mix until combined.

5. Spoon into prepared pan; spread evenly. Spread with melted chocolate.

6. Refrigerate for 20 minutes; cut into squares. Store in an airtight container in the fridge or freezer.

Norene's Notes

- Variation: For those with peanut allergies, use any other nut butter and replace chopped peanuts with a safe alternative. Almond or cashew butter work well.

- You can melt chocolate chips in a Pyrex measuring cup in the microwave, but check and stir every 30 seconds, especially if you have a powerful microwave. Microwave time is 1-2 minutes.

On busy mornings, these no-bake energy balls are lifesavers. With zero preservatives, lots of protein, and just enough chocolate and coconut to keep your sweet tooth happy, these are more like a treat than a healthy snack.

No-Bake Energy Bites

pareve · gluten-free option · freezes well · yields 15 balls

Ingredients

½ cup pumpkin seeds

½ cup sunflower seeds

¾ cup rolled oats
(gluten-free or regular)

⅓ cup mini chocolate chips

2 Tbsp unsweetened
shredded coconut

½ cup dried cranberries

½ cup slivered or
sliced almonds

1½ cups pitted Medjool
dates

1 tsp pure vanilla extract

⅓-½ cup smooth natural
peanut or almond butter

Method

1. Line a rimmed baking sheet with parchment paper. Set aside.

2. In a large bowl, combine pumpkin seeds, sunflower seeds, oats, chocolate chips, coconut, cranberries, and almonds. Mix well.

3. In a food processor fitted with the "S" blade, process dates with vanilla for 30-60 seconds, until smooth.

4. Add dates and peanut butter to seed mixture. Stir until combined.

5. Drop from a cookie scoop onto prepared baking sheet; form into bite-sized balls. Refrigerate or freeze. Store in an airtight container.

Norene's Notes

- Variation: White chocolate chips are great additions.
- Most commercial oats are processed in a facility that also process grains that contain gluten, such as wheat, barley and rye. Luckily, gluten-free oats are now available and are safe for most people with gluten intolerance.

This simple, tropical treat is a must-make summer dessert. With sweet, juicy Hawaiian flavors, it's great for barbecues and birthday parties.

Chocolate Dipped Pineapple

pareve · passover · gluten-free · do not freeze · yields 8-10 servings

Ingredients

1 bar (14 oz/400 g) semisweet chocolate, broken into chunks

1 peeled, cored pineapple, cut into ½ -inch thick rings, patted dry

Toppings

½ cup shredded coconut

½ cup slivered or sliced almonds

½ cup candy sprinkles

Method

1. Line a rimmed baking sheet with parchment paper.

2. Pour about 1 inch of water into a saucepan. Bring to a boil; reduce heat to a simmer.

3. Place chocolate into a large, dry, heatproof bowl wider than the saucepan. Place bowl over simmering water. Melt chocolate, stirring often. Cool slightly.

4. Dip half of each pineapple ring into melted chocolate, allowing excess chocolate to drip back into the bowl.

5. Arrange pineapple in a single layer on prepared baking sheet. Sprinkle with topping of choice.

6. Refrigerate for 15-20 minutes, until set. Store in an airtight container in the refrigerator. Stays fresh for 1 day.

Norene's Notes

- Be sure to pat the pineapple slices completely dry before dunking them into the melted chocolate or the chocolate will not coat them.

A fruity dessert is always a hit at bigger gatherings as well as at family dinners. This peach crisp is a lighter alternative to cakes and creamy desserts. Cinnamon, ginger, and brown sugar add warmth and spice to the fruit filling and the topping.

Brown Sugar Peach Crisp

pareve · gluten-free option · freezes well · yields 8 servings

Ingredients

Filling

8 ripe peaches, peeled and sliced (fresh or frozen) (about 7-8 cups)

⅓ cup brown sugar, lightly packed

2 Tbsp flour (regular or gluten-free)

1 Tbsp lemon juice (preferably fresh)

1 tsp ground cinnamon

¼ tsp ground ginger

Topping

1 cup flour (regular or gluten-free flour with xanthum gum)

1 cup rolled oats

½ cup brown sugar, lightly packed

1 tsp ground cinnamon

¼ tsp ground ginger

½ cup chopped pecans or almonds (optional)

⅓ cup vegetable oil

Method

1. Preheat oven to 375°F. Coat a 10-inch deep pie plate or 8 individual ramekins with nonstick cooking spray and place onto a parchment-lined rimmed baking sheet.

2. **Filling:** In a medium bowl, combine peaches with sugar, flour, lemon juice, cinnamon, and ginger. Mix well.

3. **Topping:** In a second bowl, combine topping ingredients; mix together to form crumbs.

4. Add filling mixture to prepared pie plate or divide evenly between ramekins. Sprinkle each with topping mixture.

5. Bake pie for 45-55 minutes, or ramekins for 35-40 minutes, until topping is golden and juices are bubbly. Serve warm or at room temperature.

Norene's Notes

- Variation: Instead of peaches use 6 nectarines or apricots and 2 cups fresh or frozen blueberries.
- Do-Ahead: Prepare topping ahead of time and refrigerate or freeze. When needed, prepare filling and sprinkle with topping mixture (no need to defrost it first). Bake as directed above.

Cakes

You can't beat the combination of fruit and chocolate in this fragrant cranberry loaf. Perfectly tart and sweet, it's a great cake for breakfast, brunch, or an after-dinner treat. It makes two loaves, so freeze the second one for another occasion.

Cranberry Chocolate Chip Cake

pareve · gluten-free option · freezes well · yields 2 loaves

Ingredients

3 eggs

1¼ cups sugar

1¼ cups vegetable oil

1 tsp pure vanilla extract

1½ cups orange juice

2½ cups flour
(or gluten-free flour
with xanthan gum)

1 tsp baking powder

1½ tsp baking soda

¼ tsp salt

3 cups fresh or frozen
cranberries
(no need to thaw)

1½ cups mini
chocolate chips

Method

1. Preheat oven to 350°F. Coat two 9 x 5-inch loaf pans with nonstick cooking spray.

2. In the bowl of an electric mixer fitted with the paddle attachment, beat eggs with sugar, oil, and vanilla on medium-high speed for 3-5 minutes, until light.

3. Reduce mixer speed to low; gradually blend in orange juice.

4. Add flour, baking powder, baking soda, and salt. Mix just until combined. Fold in cranberries and chocolate chips.

5. Divide batter evenly between prepared loaf pans; spread evenly. Bake for 50-60 minutes, or until a wooden toothpick inserted into the center comes out dry.

6. Allow loaves to cool for 20 minutes. Invert onto serving platters.

Norene's Notes

- Muffin Variation: In Step 5, scoop batter into muffin pans coated with nonstick spray or lined with paper liners until ¾-full. Bake at 375°F for about 25 minutes. Yields 18-24 muffins.

- Frozen cranberries don't need to be thawed. Just rinse and pat them dry with paper towels before folding them into the batter.

One of the most delicious desserts to make for company, this berry-studded Bundt cake is a tea-time essential. Fresh blueberries are layered throughout the cake, adding a burst of flavor to every bite. Sugared lemon slices make for a pretty presentation.

Blueberry Lemon Cake

pareve • gluten-free option • freezes well • yields 12-15 servings

Ingredients

4 eggs

1¼ cups sugar

1 cup vegetable oil

2 tsp pure vanilla extract

zest and juice of **2** lemons
(see Norene's Notes, below)

2¾ cups flour
(or gluten-free flour
with xantham gum)

3 tsp baking powder

1 tsp salt

2½ cups fresh blueberries
tossed with **2 Tbsp** flour
(or gluten-free flour)

Garnish

1 lemon, not peeled,
thinly sliced (discard ends
and seeds)

2 Tbsp sugar, for sprinkling

Method

1. Preheat oven to 350°F. Coat a 12-cup Bundt pan with nonstick cooking spray.

2. In the bowl of an electric mixer fitted with the paddle attachment, beat eggs with sugar, oil, and vanilla on medium-high speed for 3-5 minutes, until light. Blend in zest and lemon juice.

3. Reduce mixer speed to low; add flour, baking powder, and salt. Mix just until combined.

4. Use a rubber spatula to carefully fold in blueberries.

5. Pour batter into prepared pan; spread evenly. Gently place whole lemon slices on batter; sprinkle them lightly with sugar.

6. Bake 55-60 minutes, or until a wooden toothpick inserted into the cake comes out without any batter clinging to it.

7. Allow cake to cool. Invert cake onto a large plate; carefully invert onto a serving platter so that lemon slices are on top.

Norene's Notes

• Variation: To use frozen blueberries, thaw first; then rinse and pat dry. Instead of blueberries, substitute diced mango, peaches, or nectarines.

• Time-Saving Step: Zest and juice two lemons in advance, then slice the additional lemon for garnish.

• To test if your baking powder is still fresh, mix together ½ tsp baking powder with ½ cup hot water. If it fizzes, it's fine; otherwise, toss it.

For all my gluten-free eaters, including my daughter, I put in a delicious gluten-free cake to enjoy. This cake is flexible, as you can serve it with melted chocolate, fresh fruit, whipping cream ... whatever you like.

Light & Fluffy Chiffon Cake

pareve • passover • gluten-free • freezes well • yields 10-12 servings

Ingredients

8 eggs, separated

1 cup sugar, divided

⅓ cup vegetable oil

⅓ cup orange juice

¾ cup potato starch

Method

1. Preheat oven to 350°F. Prepare an ungreased 10-inch tube pan.

2. In an electric mixer fitted with the paddle attachment, beat egg yolks on high speed for 3-5 minutes. Gradually add ½ cup sugar; beat 3-4 minutes longer, until light and pale yellow.

3. With the motor running, slowly pour in oil and orange juice; beat 2-3 minutes longer. Gently fold in potato starch.

4. In a clean bowl, with clean beaters, beat egg whites until frothy. Gradually add remaining ½ cup sugar. Beat until stiff and glossy to form a meringue.

5. Add meringue to yolk mixture, carefully folding in until fully incorporated.

6. Gently pour batter into prepared pan. Smooth top with a spatula.

7. Bake for 1 hour. Top of cake will be golden and will spring back when lightly touched.

8. Remove from oven, immediately invert pan, and let hang until completely cool.

9. To remove cooled cake from pan, slide a flexible spatula between pan and sides of cake. Push up bottom of pan; remove sides. Carefully loosen around center tube and bottom of pan by running a thin knife blade between cake, tube, and bottom of pan. Invert cake onto a cake and then invert onto a serving platter.

Norene's Notes

- Most tube pans have 3 "legs" to stand on. If yours doesn't, invert the cake over the neck of a bottle or on a rack until cool.

If you're a chocolate lover like I am, then this beautiful tart will be a case of love at first sight. Nothing extravagant or overly complex, just flakes of sea salt sprinkled over a creamy chocolate ganache in a rich chocolate crust. Now that's simple elegance!

Salted Chocolate Ganache Tart

pareve · gluten-free option · freezes well · yields 12 servings

Ingredients

Crust

1½ cups flour (or gluten-free flour with xanthan gum)

⅓ cup unsweetened cocoa powder

⅔ cup confectioners' sugar

⅔ cup vegetable oil

1 egg

1 tsp pure vanilla extract

Ganache Filling

1 container (500 ml/2 cups) non-dairy whipping cream

1 bar (10 oz/300 g) semisweet chocolate, chopped

sea salt for sprinkling

Method

1. Preheat oven to 375°F. Lightly coat an 11-inch flan pan or pie plate with removable bottom with nonstick cooking spray.

2. **Crust:** In a large bowl, combine flour, cocoa, and confectioner's sugar. Add oil, egg, and vanilla. Mix just until dough gathers together, forming a soft dough.

3. Press dough evenly against bottom and sides of prepared pan. Bake, uncovered, for 18-20 minutes. Let cool.

4. **Ganache Filling:** In a medium saucepan, bring cream to a boil over medium-high heat. Remove pan from heat; add chocolate and stir until melted.

5. Pour ganache filling into cooled crust. Let set for 10 minutes. Sprinkle with sea salt. Refrigerate for 4 hours or overnight. Served chilled.

Norene's Notes

- Chocolate Truffle Mousse: Omit crust. Prepare filling as directed in Step 4. Refrigerate until completely cooled. Transfer to an electric mixer; whip until light. Spoon whipped mixture into individual parfait glasses. Garnish with fresh berries. Deliciously elegant!

Pie isn't usually my first pick for desserts (I'm a cake girl at heart), but a slice of this apple crumble pie is hard to resist. The cinnamon-spiced crust and warm apple filling conjure up feelings of home. Not too sweet, not too heavy, this pie is perfect for any occasion.

Apple Crumble Pie

pareve · gluten-free option · freezes well · yields 8 servings

Ingredients

Crust/Topping

3 cups flour (or gluten-free flour with xanthan gum)

1 tsp salt

½ tsp ground cinnamon

¼ cup sugar

1 cup vegetable oil

¼ cup orange juice

Filling

6 large apples (e.g., Cortland, Honeycrisp, or Granny Smith), cored, peeled, quartered, and cut into large chunks

½ cup sugar

2 tsp ground cinnamon

¼ cup lemon juice (preferably fresh)

¼ cup cinnamon-sugar (for sprinkling)

Method

1. Preheat oven to 375°F. Coat an 11-inch flan pan with a removable bottom with nonstick cooking spray.

2. **Crust/topping:** In a large bowl, combine flour, salt, cinnamon, sugar, oil, and orange juice; mix to form a crumbly mixture.

3. Remove one-third of the crumb mixture; set aside for the topping. Press remaining mixture into the bottom and up the sides of the prepared pan, forming a crust.

4. **Filling:** In a large bowl, combine apples, sugar, cinnamon, and lemon juice; mix well. Spoon evenly into crust.

5. Sprinkle reserved crumb mixture evenly over apples. Sprinkle with cinnamon-sugar.

6. Bake for 50-60 minutes, or until golden-brown. Serve hot or at room temperature.

Norene's Notes

- Test for Doneness: Pierce through the top of the pie with a sharp knife. It should slide through the apples easily and the blade should be hot to the touch when removed from pie.

I've made this pecan pie for my husband since the day we were married, and it has stood the test of time. This is his all-time favorite, so it has a special place in my heart. Sweet and crunchy, this pie has a simple, homemade feel. Try it with a scoop of ice cream on the side — yum!

Classic Pecan Pie

pareve · gluten-free option · freezes well · yields 10 servings

Ingredients

Crust

1½ cups flour
(or gluten-free flour
with xanthum gum)

¼ cup sugar

¾ cup vegetable oil

1½ Tbsp white vinegar

Filling

3 eggs

½ cup sugar

1 cup corn syrup

pinch salt

1 tsp pure vanilla extract

1½-3 cups pecan halves,
divided

Method

1. Preheat oven to 375°F. Lightly coat an 11-inch flan pan with removable bottom (or a 10-inch glass quiche dish) with nonstick cooking spray.

2. **Crust:** In a large bowl, combine flour, sugar, oil, and vinegar; mix to form a soft dough.

3. Press crust mixture evenly against bottom and sides of prepared pan (see Norene's Notes, below).

4. **Filling:** In a large bowl, combine eggs, sugar, corn syrup, salt, and vanilla. Mix well. Stir in half the pecans. Spoon filling into crust.

5. Arrange remaining pecans in a circular pattern on top of pie.

6. Bake 50-55 minutes, or until set and edges of crust are golden brown. Let cool before serving.

Norene's Notes

- Place pie plate on a foil-lined rimmed baking sheet to catch any spills.
- Variation: Chocolate Pecan Pie: Add 1 cup chocolate chips to filling along with pecans.
- Go Nuts: Pecans have a natural sweetness. Store them in the refrigerator or freezer for maximum freshness.

It's the little details that give each chocolate cake recipe a different kind of magic. Here, it's the zucchini. Slivers of healthful squash give the cake outstanding moistness and sweetness, while walnuts add texture, flavor, and beauty to this cake.

Chocolate Zucchini Cake

pareve • gluten-free option • freezes well • yields 12 servings

Ingredients

3 eggs

¾ cup vegetable oil

1 cup granulated sugar

1 cup brown sugar

1 tsp pure vanilla extract

½ cup orange juice

3 cups grated zucchini

2½ cups flour
(or gluten-free flour
with xantham gum)

½ cup unsweetened
cocoa powder

2½ tsp baking powder

1½ tsp baking soda

pinch salt

1 cup walnuts

Method

1. Preheat oven to 350°F. Coat a 12-cup Bundt pan with nonstick cooking spray.

2. In the bowl of an electric mixer fitted with the paddle attachment, beat eggs with oil, sugars, and vanilla on medium-high speed for 3-5 minutes, until light. Reduce mixer speed to low; gradually blend in orange juice and zucchini.

3. Add flour, cocoa, baking powder, baking soda, and salt. Mix just until combined.

4. Pour batter into prepared pan; spread evenly. Sprinkle with walnuts.

5. Bake 50-60 minutes or until a wooden toothpick inserted into the center comes out without any batter clinging to it.

6. Allow cake to cool. Invert cake onto a large plate; carefully invert onto a serving platter so walnuts are on top.

Norene's Notes

- Chocolate Zucchini Muffins: Prepare batter as directed above. Scoop batter into lined muffin pan cups, filling compartments two-thirds full. Bake at 375°F for 25-30 minutes, until nicely browned.

Combining the fabulous flavors of fall, this cake is beyond delicious and an absolute must-try for Succot or Thanksgiving. This cake is super moist and the crumbly, sweet topping adds a simple, elegant touch.

Crumb Topped Pumpkin Cake

pareve · gluten-free option · freezes well · yields 12 servings

Ingredients

4 eggs

¾ cup vegetable oil

1 cup brown sugar, lightly packed

½ cup granulated sugar

1 tsp pure vanilla extract

1 can (15 oz/425 g) pumpkin puree

3 cups flour (or gluten-free flour with xanthum gum)

1 tsp baking powder

½ tsp baking soda

¼ tsp salt

2 tsp ground cinnamon

¾ cup orange juice

Topping

⅔ cup flour (or gluten-free flour with xanthum gum)

⅓ cup brown sugar, lightly packed

1 tsp ground cinnamon

3 Tbsp vegetable oil

Method

1. Preheat oven to 350°F. Coat a Bundt pan with nonstick cooking spray.

2. In the bowl of an electric mixer fitted with the paddle attachment, beat eggs with oil, sugars, and vanilla on medium-high speed for 3-5 minutes, until light.

3. Reduce mixer speed to low; gradually blend in pumpkin puree.

4. Add flour, baking powder, baking soda, salt, and cinnamon to a medium bowl; stir to combine.

5. Alternately add dry ingredients and orange juice to batter, starting and ending with dry ingredients. Mix just until combined. Pour batter into prepared pan; spread evenly.

6. **Topping:** In a medium bowl, combine flour, sugar, cinnamon, and oil, mixing well to form crumbs. Sprinkle evenly over batter.

7. Bake for 50-60 minutes, or until a wooden toothpick inserted into the center comes out without any batter clinging to it.

8. Cool cake for 15-20 minutes. Invert cake onto a large flat plate, then carefully invert onto a serving platter so topping is on top. Some of the crumbs will fall off; just sprinkle them back on top.

Norene's Notes

- Variation: Add ½ cup chopped nuts to the topping mixture.
- Simple Elegance: Drizzle caramel sauce in a zigzag design over cooled cake.

This easy ice-cream dessert is the perfect way to end a meal in the hot summer months. The unexpected addition of a crumbly granola-type crust and topping give the cake a sophisticated look while helping to keep its integrity even when the ice cream starts to soften.

Granola Ice Cream Cake

dairy · pareve option · gluten-free option · freezes well · yields 12 servings

Ingredients

8 cups store-bought ice cream (dairy or pareve) (see Norene's Notes, below)

1½ cups flour (or gluten-free flour with xanthan gum)

1 cup rolled oats (regular or gluten-free)

½ cup brown sugar, lightly packed

1 tsp ground cinnamon

½ cup vegetable oil

1 cup chopped pecans (optional)

2 cups mini chocolate chips

Method

1. To soften ice cream without melting it, transfer the container from the freezer to the refrigerator for 20-30 minutes before using (or let stand at room temperature for 10-15 minutes).

2. Preheat oven to 350°F. Line a rimmed baking sheet with parchment paper.

3. In a large bowl, combine flour, oats, brown sugar, cinnamon, oil, and pecans, if using; stir to combine.

4. Spread evenly on prepared baking sheet; bake for 15-20 minutes, until golden, stirring occasionally. Cool completely.

5. Stir in chocolate chips; divide mixture in half.

6. Spoon half the softened ice cream into a 9- or 10-inch springform pan. Sprinkle with half the granola mixture. Spoon on the remaining ice cream; spread evenly. Sprinkle with remaining granola, pressing it down so it adheres to the ice cream. Cover; freeze.

Norene's Notes

- This dessert can also be made in a 9 x 13-inch Pyrex baking dish. Try it with different flavors of ice cream. Different every time!
- Easy Elegance: Prepare topping mixture in advance; store in an airtight container in the refrigerator or freezer. Just before serving, layer topping and scoops of ice cream in parfait glasses. Top with whipped cream; drizzle with chocolate or caramel sauce. Serve immediately.

This luscious pie is a recipe from my mother-in-law, Bonny Silver; it's a staple in my husband's family. As kids, Jeffery and his brother Jeremy would sneak "test tastes" of the pie, and they still try this trick today. I love that tradition — and this pie. The classics are classics for a reason.

Key Lime Pie

dairy · gluten-free option · freezes well · yields 8 servings

Ingredients

Crust

1½ cups graham crackers crumbs (regular or gluten-free)

2 Tbsp brown sugar, lightly packed

⅓ cup melted butter

Filling

2 cans (14 oz/389 ml each) sweetened condensed milk

½ cup sour cream (regular or light)

1½ Tbsp key lime zest

¾ cup key lime juice (see Norene's Notes, below)

additional zest, for garnishing

Method

1. Preheat oven to 350°F. Coat a 10-inch glass or ceramic quiche dish with nonstick cooking spray.

2. **Crust:** In a medium bowl, combine graham cracker crumbs with sugar and butter; mix well. Press crumb mixture evenly into bottom of prepared pan.

3. Bake, uncovered, for 8-10 minutes, until golden.

4. **Filling:** Meanwhile, in a second bowl, combine condensed milk, sour cream, lime zest, and juice; mix well.

5. Pour filling into parbaked crust. Bake, uncovered, for 8-10 minutes, until set. Let cool completely.

6. Chill for at least 3 hours before serving. Garnish with additional lime zest.

Norene's Notes

- Key limes are much smaller than regular limes and are slightly less tart. You can buy bottled lime juice, but fresh provides superior results. If you use regular limes, then your pie will not be "key lime pie!"
- Shopping Tip: You'll need 20-24 fresh key limes to make ¾ cup juice.
- Shortcut: Use a prepared graham cracker crust.
- Over-the-Top Variation: Garnish pie with swirls of sweetened whipped cream.

Understated and elegant, this easy, elegant cheesecake will take you by surprise. It's the perfect dessert to serve for Shavuot or Chanukah.

Raspberry Swirl White Chocolate Cheesecake

dairy · gluten-free option · freezes well · yields 12-15 servings

Ingredients

Crust

1½ cups graham cracker crumbs (regular or gluten free) (18-24 crackers)

2 Tbsp brown sugar, lightly packed

⅓ cup melted butter

Filling

4 bars (8 oz/250 g each) cream cheese, cut into chunks, at room temperature

1¼ cups sugar

3 Tbsp lemon juice (preferably fresh)

4 eggs

2 cups white chocolate chips, melted

½ cup strawberry or raspberry jam

Method

1. Preheat oven to 325°F. Coat bottom and sides of a 10-inch springform pan with nonstick cooking spray.

2. **Crust:** In a medium bowl, combine crumbs with sugar and butter; mix well. Press crumb mixture evenly into prepared pan. Bake for 10 minutes, until golden.

3. **Filling:** In the bowl of an electric mixer or food processor, beat cream cheese and sugar until light. Add lemon juice and eggs; beat until smooth and creamy, scraping down sides of bowl as needed.

4. Fold in white chocolate. Pour batter over crust.

5. Fill a pie plate halfway with water and place on bottom rack in oven. Place cheesecake on middle rack. Bake for 45-55 minutes. When done, edges will be set, but the center 2 inches will jiggle slightly.

6. Turn off heat, prop oven door partially open with a wooden spoon, and let cheesecake cool in oven for about 45 minutes to finish baking and firm up.

7. Cover; refrigerate for several hours or overnight.

8. Shortly before serving, heat jam; swirl jam over cheesecake.

Norene's Notes

- Mini Variation: Prepare filling as directed. Omit crust. Line 24 muffin pan cups with paper liners. Place a chocolate cookie into each liner. Top with filling. Drop a teaspoonful of jam onto each mini cheesecake; swirl with a toothpick. Bake in preheated 350°F oven for 10-12 minutes, until set. Garnish cooled mini cheesecakes with chocolate shavings.

Nutritional Information

The nutritional analysis was calculated using data from ESHA (The Food Processor SQL Edition 10.14.2) and, when necessary, manufacturers' food labels.

- Values given for each recipe are per serving unless stated otherwise

- When there is a choice of ingredients, the first ingredient was analyzed. The analysis does not include optional ingredients or those with no specified amounts.

- The smaller measure of an ingredient was analyzed when a range is given (e.g., ¼ cup was analyzed when a recipe calls for ¼-⅓ cup).

- The nutrient values have been rounded off for carbohydrates, fiber, fat, calories, protein, cholesterol, sodium, potassium, iron, calcium, and phosphorus.

- The phosphorus content included in the analysis is helpful for people with medical problems, including kidney disease.

- A serving of at least 2 grams of fiber is considered a moderate source, 4 grams is a high source, and 6 grams is considered a very high source of fiber.

- When cheese is called for, the recipe was analyzed using lower fat or reduced fat cheeses, unless otherwise indicated.

- When sour cream or yogurt is called for, the recipe was analyzed using lower fat versions, unless otherwise indicated.

- When milk is called for, the recipe was analyzed using 1% milk, unless otherwise indicated.

- When eggs are called for, the recipe was analyzed using large eggs.

- Specific measurements of salt were included in the analysis (e.g., 1 tsp salt). When a recipe does not give a specific measurement (e.g., salt to taste), then salt was not included in the analysis. To reduce sodium content, choose low-sodium or salt-free products. Note that sodium content varies by brand of soy or tamari sauce; the sodium content of your dish may vary from the amount listed in this directory.

- Garnishes were not calculated, unless a specific amount is indicated.

- To keep your recipes gluten-free, use gluten-free soy sauce or tamari.

- To keep your recipes dairy-free, use rice, soy, unsweetened almond, or coconut milk.

Appetizers

Beets & Avocado *p. 26*
Calories: 267 kcal
Carbs: 22 g (14 g sugar, 6 g of fiber)
Protein: 4 g
Fat: 21 g (3 g saturated)
Cholesterol: 0 mg
Potassium: 284 mg
Calcium: 34 mg
Sodium: 64 mg
Iron: 2 mg

Colorful Chickpea Salad *p. 22*
Calories: 329 kcal
Carbs: 37 g (4 g sugar, 9 g of fiber)
Protein: 12 g
Fat: 14 g (2 g saturated)
Cholesterol: 0 mg
Potassium: 502 mg
Calcium: 102 mg
Sodium: 49 mg
Iron: 3 mg

Deli-Wrapped Pretzels *p. 32*
Calories: 187 kcal
Carbs: 22 g (7 g sugar, 1 g of fiber)
Protein: 17 g
Fat: 5 g (2 g saturated)
Cholesterol: 39 mg
Potassium: 9 mg
Calcium: 1 mg
Sodium: 987 mg
Iron: 2 mg

Fresh Fig & Tomato Salad *p. 16*
Calories: 178 kcal
Carbs: 24 g (20 g sugar, 4 g of fiber)
Protein: 2 g
Fat: 10 g (1 g saturated)
Cholesterol: 0 mg
Potassium: 453 mg
Calcium: 52 mg
Sodium: 7 mg
Iron: 1 mg

Hoisin Steak Bites *p. 34*
Calories: 718 kcal
Carbs: 22 g (16 g sugar, 1 g of fiber)
Protein: 109 g
Fat: 18 g (6 g saturated)
Cholesterol: 271 mg
Potassium: 1090 mg
Calcium: 35 mg
Sodium: 623 mg
Iron: 10 mg

Pulled BBQ Beef Nachos *p. 30*
Calories: 707 kcal
Carbs: 78 g (17 g sugar, 6 g of fiber)
Protein: 49 g
Fat: 23 g (6 g saturated)
Cholesterol: 128 mg
Potassium: 1144 mg
Calcium: 164 mg
Sodium: 595 mg
Iron: 6 mg

Roasted Eggplant Salad *p. 18*
Calories: 93 kcal
Carbs: 12 (6 g sugar, 6 g of fiber)
Protein: 2 g
Fat: 5 g (1 g saturated)
Cholesterol: 0 mg
Potassium: 473 mg
Calcium: 30 mg
Sodium: 329 mg
Iron: 1 mg

Smoked Salmon Salad *p. 28*
Calories: 462 kcal
Carbs: 28 g (14 g sugar, 6 g of fiber)
Protein: 27 g
Fat: 31 g (5 g saturated)
Cholesterol: 58 mg
Potassium: 551 mg
Calcium: 137 mg
Sodium: 810 mg
Iron: 6 mg

Stuffed Avocados *p. 36*
Calories: 240 kcal
Carbs: 11 g (1 g sugar, 6 g of fiber)
Protein: 16 g
Fat: 18 g (4 g saturated)
Cholesterol: 33 mg
Potassium: 56 mg
Calcium: 5 mg
Sodium: 391 mg
Iron: 2 mg

Sweet Potato Quinoa Patties *p. 20*
Calories: 82 kcal
Carbs: 11 g (1 g sugar, 1 g of fiber)
Protein: 3 g
Fat: 3 g (1 g saturated)
Cholesterol: 41 mg
Potassium: 56 mg
Calcium: 19 mg
Sodium: 164 mg
Iron: 1 mg

Tomato Flowers With Guacamole *p. 14*
Calories: 145 kcal
Carbs: 14 g (8 g sugar, 4 g of fiber)
Protein: 2 g
Fat: 11 g (2 g saturated)
Cholesterol: 0 mg
Potassium: 465 mg
Calcium: 26 mg
Sodium: 55 mg
Iron: 1 mg

Updated Israeli Salad *p. 24*
Calories: 136 kcal
Carbs: 11 g (6 g sugar, 3 g of fiber)
Protein: 2 g
Fat: 12 g (2 g saturated)
Cholesterol: 0 mg
Potassium: 361 mg
Calcium: 58 mg
Sodium: 546 mg
Iron: 1 mg

Watermelon Radish & Cucumber Salad *p. 12*
Calories: 176 kcal
Carbs: 23 g (15 g sugar, 5 g of fiber)
Protein: 3 g
Fat: 10 g (2 g saturated)
Cholesterol: 0 mg
Potassium: 809 mg
Calcium: 92 mg
Sodium: 54 mg
Iron: 2 mg

Soups

Black Bean & Tomato Soup *p. 40*
Calories: 176 kcal
Carbs: 29 g (5 g sugar, 9 g of fiber)
Protein: 9 g
Fat: 3 g (0 g saturated)
Cholesterol: 0 mg
Potassium: 549 mg
Calcium: 105 mg
Sodium: 528 mg
Iron: 3 mg

Cheesy Potato Leek Soup *p. 58*
Calories: 172 kcal
Carbs: 31 g (3 g sugar, 3 g of fiber)
Protein: 6 g
Fat: 3 G (1 g saturated)
Cholesterol: 3 mg
Potassium: 526 mg
Calcium: 103 mg
Sodium: 636 mg
Iron: 1 mg

Mushroom Cauliflower Soup p. 50

Calories: 63 kcal

Carbs: 10 g (4 g sugar, 3 g of fiber)

Protein: 4 g

Fat: 2 G (0 g saturated)

Cholesterol: 0 mg

Potassium: 590 mg

Calcium: 46 mg

Sodium: 523 mg

Iron: 1 mg

Pumpkin Soup With Pumpkin Crunch p. 54

Calories: 213 kcal

Carbs: 25 g (11 g sugar, 6 g of fiber)

Protein: 7 g

Fat: 11 g (2 g saturated)

Cholesterol: 0 mg

Potassium: 370 mg

Calcium: 60 mg

Sodium: 512 mg

Iron: 3 mg

Roasted Cauliflower & Chickpea Soup p. 52

Calories: 145 kcal

Carbs: 21 g (5 g sugar, 5 g of fiber)

Protein: 6 g

Fat: 4 g (1 g saturated)

Cholesterol: 0 mg

Potassium: 405 mg

Calcium: 65 mg

Sodium: 47 mg

Iron: 1 mg

Squash & Leek Soup p. 42

Calories: 141 kcal

Carbs: 28 g (14 g sugar, 4 g of fiber)

Protein: 2 g

Fat: 4 g (1 g saturated)

Cholesterol: 0 mg

Potassium: 459 mg

Calcium: 82 mg

Sodium: 260 mg

Iron: 1 mg

Strawberry Orange Soup p. 46

Calories: 58 kcal

Carbs: 15 g (12 g sugar, 2 g of fiber)

Protein: 1 g

Fat: 0 g (0 g saturated)

Cholesterol: 0 mg

Potassium: 157 mg

Calcium: 17 mg

Sodium: 3 mg

Iron: 0 mg

Sweet Potato & Kale Soup p. 44

Calories: 113 kcal

Carbs: 21 g (6 g sugar, 4 g of fiber)

Protein: 3 g

Fat: 2 g (0 g saturated)

Cholesterol: 0 mg

Potassium: 260 mg

Calcium: 43 mg

Sodium: 182 mg

Iron: 1 mg

Thick & Hearty Split Pea Soup p. 60

Calories: 186 kcal

Carbs: 30 g (5 g sugar, 11 g of fiber)

Protein: 10 g

Fat: 4 g (1 g saturated)

Cholesterol: 0 mg

Potassium: 448 mg

Calcium: 41 mg

Sodium: 513 mg

Iron: 2 mg

Tomato Quinoa Soup p. 56

Calories: 104 kcal

Carbs: 19 g (6 g sugar, 3 g of fiber)

Protein: 2 g

Fat: 3 g (0 g saturated)

Cholesterol: 0 mg

Potassium: 293 mg

Calcium: 48 mg

Sodium: 280 mg

Iron: 1 mg

Zucchini Dill Soup p. 48

Calories: 71 kcal

Carbs: 12 (7 g sugar, 3 g of fiber)

Protein: 3 g

Fat: 2 g (0 g saturated)

Cholesterol: 0 mg

Potassium: 626 mg

Calcium: 52 mg

Sodium: 513 mg

Iron: 1 mg

Salads

Balsamic Spinach Salad With Caramelized Onions p. 84

Calories: 181 kcal

Carbs: 14 g (8 g sugar, 4 g of fiber)

Protein: 3 g

Fat: 14 g (2 g saturated)

Cholesterol: 0 mg

Potassium: 120 mg

Calcium: 68 mg

Sodium: 51 mg

Iron: 2 mg

Blueberry Cabbage Slaw p. 76

Calories: 202 kcal

Carbs: 27 g (16 g sugar, 5 g of fiber)

Protein: 3 g

Fat: 11 g (2 g saturated)

Cholesterol: 0 mg

Potassium: 411 mg

Calcium: 67 mg

Sodium: 317 mg

Iron: 1 mg

Cauliflower Salad p. 82

Calories: 130 kcal

Carbs: 18 g (9 g sugar, 5 g of fiber)

Protein: 4 g

Fat: 8 g (1 g saturated)

Cholesterol: 10 mg

Potassium: 607 mg

Calcium: 51 mg

Sodium: 784 mg

Iron: 1 mg

Crisp Summer Salad p. 66

Calories: 223 kcal

Carbs: 33 g (19 g sugar, 4 g of fiber)

Protein: 4 g

Fat: 10 g (2 g saturated)

Cholesterol: 0 mg

Potassium: 340 mg

Calcium: 52 mg

Sodium: 29 mg

Iron: 2 mg

Edamame & Radish Salad p. 64

Calories: 168 kcal

Carbs: 15 g (9 g sugar, 3 g of fiber)

Protein: 6 g

Fat: 11 g (2 g saturated)

Cholesterol: 0 mg

Potassium: 283 mg

Calcium: 95 mg

Sodium: 579 mg

Iron: 2 mg

Everything Kale Salad p. 70

Calories: 243 kcal

Carbs: 38 g (22 g sugar, 7 g of fiber)

Protein: 4 g

Fat: 10 g (1 g saturated)

Cholesterol: 0 mg

Potassium: 483 mg

Calcium: 127 mg

Sodium: 60 mg

Iron: 2 mg

Four-Bean Salad
With Poppy Seed Dressing *p. 92*
Calories: 306 kcal
Carbs: 39 g (13 g sugar, 11 g of fiber)
Protein: 12 g
Fat: 13 g (2 g saturated)
Cholesterol: 0 mg
Potassium: 571 mg
Calcium: 152 mg
Sodium: 548 mg
Iron: 3 mg

Kale & Roasted Chickpea
Salad *p. 72*
Calories: 232 kcal
Carbs: 21 g (3 g sugar, 7 g of fiber)
Protein: 10 g
Fat: 13 g (2 g saturated)
Cholesterol: 0 mg
Potassium: 470 mg
Calcium: 155 mg
Sodium: 222 mg
Iron: 2 mg

Marinated Artichoke Salad *p. 74*
Calories: 322 kcal
Carbs: 22 g (13 g sugar, 3 g of fiber)
Protein: 3 g
Fat: 23 g (4 g saturated)
Cholesterol: 0 mg
Potassium: 116 mg
Calcium: 33 mg
Sodium: 796 mg
Iron: 1 mg

Marvelous Marinated Salad *p. 68*
Calories: 241 kcal
Carbs: 28 g (14 g sugar, 4 g of fiber)
Protein: 4 g
Fat: 13 g (2 g saturated)
Cholesterol: 0 mg
Potassium: 278 mg
Calcium: 54 mg
Sodium: 858 mg
Iron: 1 mg

Mother's Day Cabbage Salad *p. 78*
Calories: 276 kcal
Carbs: 35 g (26 g sugar, 8 g of fiber)
Protein: 3 g
Fat: 16 g (2 g saturated)
Cholesterol: 0 mg
Potassium: 173 mg
Calcium: 111 mg
Sodium: 33 mg
Iron: 1 mg

Pomegranate & Persimmon
Salad *p. 86*
Calories: 311 kcal
Carbs: 31 g (22 g sugar, 5 g of fiber)
Protein: 5 g
Fat: 21 g (2 g saturated)
Cholesterol: 0 mg
Potassium: 352 mg
Calcium: 122 mg
Sodium: 15 mg
Iron: 2 mg

Spinach Pasta Salad *p. 88*
Calories: 220 kcal
Carbs: 33 g (20 g sugar, 3 g of fiber)
Protein: 3 g
Fat: 10 G (1 g saturated)
Cholesterol: 0 mg
Potassium: 56 mg
Calcium: 63 mg
Sodium: 476 mg
Iron: 2 mg

Strawberry Star Fruit Salad *p. 90*
Calories: 199 kcal
Carbs: 20 g (14 g sugar, 3 g of fiber)
Protein: 2 g
Fat: 14 g (2 g saturated)
Cholesterol: 0 mg
Potassium: 40 mg
Calcium: 37 mg
Sodium: 36 mg
Iron: 2 mg

Two-Toned Zucchini & Mushroom
Salad *p. 80*
Calories: 175 kcal
Carbs: 15 g (10 g sugar, 3 g of fiber)
Protein: 3 g
Fat: 13 g (2 g saturated)
Cholesterol: 0 mg
Potassium: 541 mg
Calcium: 37 mg
Sodium: 399 mg
Iron: 1 mg

Fish

Almond-Crusted Fish Sticks *p. 114*
Calories: 447 kcal
Carbs: 8 g (1 g sugar, 4 g of fiber)
Protein: 41 g
Fat: 29 g (3 g saturated)
Cholesterol: 78 mg
Potassium: 623 mg
Calcium: 78 mg
Sodium: 621 mg
Iron: 2 mg

Basil Salmon
With Sun-Dried Tomatoes *p. 104*
Calories: 232 kcal
Carbs: 10 g (8 g sugar, 1 g of fiber)
Protein: 32 g
Fat: 7 g (1 g saturated)
Cholesterol: 70 mg
Potassium: 799 mg
Calcium: 25 mg
Sodium: 121 mg
Iron: 1 mg

Candied Cashew Salmon *p. 98*
Calories: 355 kcal
Carbs: 18 g (9 g sugar, 2 g of fiber)
Protein: 35 g
Fat: 17 g (3 g saturated)
Cholesterol: 70 mg
Potassium: 682 mg
Calcium: 21 mg
Sodium: 117 mg
Iron: 2 mg

Chili Lime Fish Fillets *p. 116*
Calories: 218 kcal
Carbs: 4 g (0 g sugar, 1 g of fiber)
Protein: 35 g
Fat: 8 g (2 g saturated)
Cholesterol: 85 mg
Potassium: 585 mg
Calcium: 30 mg
Sodium: 255 mg
Iron: 1 mg

Garlic & Tomato Fish Fillets *p. 112*
Calories: 240 kcal
Carbs: 11 g (2 g sugar, 2 g of fiber)
Protein: 29 g
Fat: 9 g (2 g saturated)
Cholesterol: 82 mg
Potassium: 676 mg
Calcium: 88 mg
Sodium: 263 mg
Iron: 2 mg

Honey Garlic Herbed Salmon *p. 96*
Calories: 352 kcal
Carbs: 18 g (15 g sugar, 0 g of fiber)
Protein: 36 g
Fat: 15 g (2 g saturated)
Cholesterol: 78 mg
Potassium: 658 mg
Calcium: 29 mg
Sodium: 915 mg
Iron: 1 mg

Lemon Sea Bass in Parchment Packets *p. 108*

Calories: 184 kcal
Carbs: 5 g (2 g sugar, 1 g of fiber)
Protein: 32 g
Fat: 4 g (1 g saturated)
Cholesterol: 70 mg
Potassium: 608 mg
Calcium: 39 mg
Sodium: 123 mg
Iron: 1 mg

One-Dish Salmon, Mushrooms & Peppers *p. 100*

Calories: 329 kcal
Carbs: 18 g (14 g sugar, 3 g of fiber)
Protein: 38 g
Fat: 11 g (2 g saturated)
Cholesterol: 78 mg
Potassium: 1074 mg
Calcium: 29 mg
Sodium: 423 mg
Iron: 2 mg

Pan-Fried Fillets & Pickled Onions *p. 106*

Calories: 254 kcal
Carbs: 10 g (9 g sugar, 0 g of fiber)
Protein: 32 g
Fat: 9 g (1 g saturated)
Cholesterol: 83 mg
Potassium: 775 mg
Calcium: 19 mg
Sodium: 598 mg
Iron: 0 mg

Roasted Red Pepper Salmon *p. 102*

Calories: 242 kcal
Carbs: 6 g (3 g sugar, 1 g of fiber)
Protein: 36 g
Fat: 8 g (1 g saturated)
Cholesterol: 78 mg
Potassium: 653 mg
Calcium: 26 mg
Sodium: 313 mg
Iron: 1 mg

Roasted Tomato Fish Fillets *p. 110*

Calories: 219 kcal
Carbs: 3 g (2 g sugar, 1 g of fiber)
Protein: 35 g
Fat: 8 g (2 g saturated)
Cholesterol: 85 mg
Potassium: 686 mg
Calcium: 39 mg
Sodium: 92 mg
Iron: 1 mg

Poultry

Chicken & Quinoa Salad *p. 126*

Calories: 378 kcal
Carbs: 37 g (19 g sugar, 4 g of fiber)
Protein: 25 g
Fat: 15 g (2 g saturated)
Cholesterol: 65 mg
Potassium: 367 mg
Calcium: 39 mg
Sodium: 105 mg
Iron: 2 mg

Chicken Italiano *p. 148*

Calories: 344 kcal
Carbs: 17 g (10 g sugar, 4 g of fiber)
Protein: 42 g
Fat: 12 g (2 g saturated)
Cholesterol: 129 mg
Potassium: 1166 mg
Calcium: 82 mg
Sodium: 101 mg
Iron: 3 mg

Chicken Packets With Spinach & Peppers *p. 122*

Calories: 288 kcal
Carbs: 8 g (2 g sugar, 3 g of fiber)
Protein: 29 g
Fat: 15 g (2 g saturated)
Cholesterol: 86 mg
Potassium: 579 mg
Calcium: 75 mg
Sodium: 421 mg
Iron: 3 mg

Flaked Quinoa Schnitzel *p. 134*

Calories: 269 kcal
Carbs: 19 g (2 g sugar, 2 g of fiber)
Protein: 32 g
Fat: 6 g (1 g saturated)
Cholesterol: 161 mg
Potassium: 419mg
Calcium: 22 mg
Sodium: 84 mg
Iron: 2 mg

Grilled Chicken

With Avocado Cucumber Salsa *p. 120*

Calories: 266 kcal
Carbs: 11 g (4 g sugar, 4 g of fiber)
Protein: 29 g
Fat: 12 g (2 g saturated)
Cholesterol: 86 mg
Potassium: 519 mg
Calcium: 112 mg
Sodium: 75 mg
Iron: 12 mg

With Mango Salsa *p. 120*

Calories: 242 kcal
Carbs: 15 g (13 g sugar, 2 g of fiber)
Protein: 28 g
Fat: 8 g (1 g saturated)
Cholesterol: 86 mg
Potassium: 512 mg
Calcium: 23 mg
Sodium: 56 mg
Iron: 1 mg

With Tomato Olive Salsa *p. 120*

Calories: 262 kcal
Carbs: 8 g (4 g sugar, 1 g of fiber)
Protein: 27 g
Fat: 14 g (2 g saturated)
Cholesterol: 86 mg
Potassium: 517 mg
Calcium: 24 mg
Sodium: 226 mg
Iron: 1 mg

Grilled Chicken Burgers *p. 132*

Calories: 132 kcal
Carbs: 2 g (1 g sugar, 1 g of fiber)
Protein: 27 g
Fat: 2 g (0 g saturated)
Cholesterol: 65 mg
Potassium: 63 mg
Calcium: 16 mg
Sodium: 349 mg
Iron: 1 mg

Honey-Roasted Pistachio Chicken *p. 146*

(4 servings)

Calories: 749 kcal
Carbs: 60 g (50 g sugar, 3 g of fiber)
Protein: 79 g
Fat: 21 g (4 g saturated)
Cholesterol: 238 mg
Potassium: 1098 mg
Calcium: 97 mg
Sodium: 853 mg
Iron: 5 mg

(6 servings)

Calories: 499 kcal
Carbs: 40 g (34 g sugar, 2 g of fiber)
Protein: 53 g
Fat: 14 g (3 g saturated)
Cholesterol: 159 mg
Potassium: 732 mg
Calcium: 64 mg
Sodium: 569 mg
Iron: 3 mg

Honey Sriracha Chicken *p. 136*

(4 servings)
Calories: 584 kcal
Carbs: 26 g (22 g sugar, 1 g of fiber)
Protein: 75 g
Fat: 19 g (4 g saturated)
Cholesterol: 238 mg
Potassium: 830 mg
Calcium: 60 mg
Sodium: 661 mg
Iron: 3 mg

(6 servings)
Calories: 389 kcal
Carbs: 18 g (15 g sugar, 0 g of fiber)
Protein: 50 g
Fat: 13 g (3 g saturated)
Cholesterol: 159 mg
Potassium: 553 mg
Calcium: 40 mg
Sodium: 440 mg
Iron: 2 mg

Maple Cinnamon Chicken *p. 140*

(4 servings)
Calories: 546 kcal
Carbs: 35 g (22 g sugar, 3 g of fiber)
Protein: 74 g
Fat: 11 g (3 g saturated)
Cholesterol: 238 mg
Potassium: 1060 mg
Calcium: 107 mg
Sodium: 309 mg
Iron: 4 mg

(6 servings)
Calories: 364 kcal
Carbs: 23 g (15 g sugar, 2 g of fiber)
Protein: 49 g
Fat: 7 g (2 g saturated)
Cholesterol: 159 mg
Potassium: 707 mg
Calcium: 71 mg
Sodium: 205 mg
Iron: 3 mg

Nectarine Chicken *p. 142*

(4 servings)
Calories: 599 kcal
Carbs: 40 g (35 g sugar, 2 g of fiber)
Protein: 74 g
Fat: 11 g (3 g saturated)
Cholesterol: 238 mg
Potassium: 1060 mg
Calcium: 82 mg
Sodium: 272 mg
Iron: 4 mg

(6 servings)
Calories: 400 kcal
Carbs: 27 g (23 g sugar, 1 g of fiber)
Protein: 49 g
Fat: 7 g (2 g saturated)
Cholesterol: 159 mg
Potassium: 706 mg
Calcium: 55 mg
Sodium: 181 mg
Iron: 2 mg

Pesto Chicken *p. 124*
Calories: 486 kcal
Carbs: 5 g (1 g sugar, 2 g of fiber)
Protein: 43 g
Fat: 33 g (5 g saturated)
Cholesterol: 129 mg
Potassium: 653 mg
Calcium: 66 mg
Sodium: 571 mg
Iron: 2 mg

Red Wine Chicken & Potatoes *p. 138*
Calories: 608 kcal
Carbs: 40 g (29 g sugar, 2 g of fiber)
Protein: 75 g
Fat: 11 G (3 g saturated)
Cholesterol: 238 mg
Potassium: 1036 mg
Calcium: 63 mg
Sodium: 275 mg
Iron: 5 mg

Roast Turkey With Strawberry Pineapple Salsa *p. 130*
Calories: 386 kcal
Carbs: 23 g (17 g sugar, 3 g of fiber)
Protein: 54 g
Fat: 7 g (1 g saturated)
Cholesterol: 130 mg
Potassium: 647 mg
Calcium: 58 mg
Sodium: 499 mg
Iron: 2 mg

Smoked Turkey Cabbage Slaw *p. 128*
Calories: 344 kcal
Carbs: 31 g (24 g sugar, 5 g of fiber)
Protein: 29 g
Fat: 9 g (1 g saturated)
Cholesterol: 60 mg
Potassium: 61 mg
Calcium: 46 mg
Sodium: 1506 mg
Iron: 6 mg

Yum Drums *p. 144*

(4 servings)
Calories: 521 kcal
Carbs: 25 g (20 g sugar, 1 g of fiber)
Protein: 72 g
Fat: 14 g (4 g saturated)
Cholesterol: 326 mg
Potassium: 944 mg
Calcium: 50 mg
Sodium: 711 mg
Iron: 3 mg

(6 servings)
Calories: 348 kcal
Carbs: 16 g (13 g sugar, 1 g of fiber)
Protein: 48 g
Fat: 9 g (2 g saturated)
Cholesterol: 217 mg
Potassium: 629 mg
Calcium: 34 mg
Sodium: 474 mg
Iron: 2 mg

Meat

Asian-Flavored Miami Ribs *p. 158*
Calories: 340 kcal
Carbs: 19 g (15 g sugar, 1 g of fiber)
Protein: 24 g
Fat: 19 g (6 g saturated)
Cholesterol: 67 mg
Potassium: 457 mg
Calcium: 20 mg
Sodium: 842 mg
Iron: 3 mg

Balsamic Glazed Strawberry Ribs *p. 162*
Calories: 223 kcal
Carbs: 29 g (10 g sugar, 1 g of fiber)
Protein: 15 g
Fat: 8 g (3 g saturated)
Cholesterol: 45 mg
Potassium: 347 mg
Calcium: 18 mg
Sodium: 51 mg
Iron: 2 mg

Corned Beef & Herbs *p. 166*
Calories: 372 kcal
Carbs: 5 g (4 g sugar, 0 g of fiber)
Protein: 47 g
Fat: 17 g (6 g saturated)
Cholesterol: 141 mg
Potassium: 784 mg
Calcium: 20 mg
Sodium: 182 mg
Iron: 5 mg

Deli Hash *p. 160*
Calories: 323 kcal
Carbs: 40 g (3 g sugar, 4 g of fiber)
Protein: 16 g
Fat: 12 g (3 g saturated)
Cholesterol: 33 mg
Potassium: 1237 mg
Calcium: 30 mg
Sodium: 764 mg
Iron: 2 mg

Green Bean & Corned Beef Salad *p. 168*
Calories: 581 kcal
Carbs: 38 g (27 g sugar, 4 g of fiber)
Protein: 56 g
Fat: 27 g (8 g saturated)
Cholesterol: 146 mg
Potassium: 213 mg
Calcium: 38 mg
Sodium: 2234 mg
Iron: 7 mg

Grilled Skirt Steak *p. 152*
Calories: 547 kcal
Carbs: 12 g (8 g sugar, 1 g of fiber)
Protein: 62 g
Fat: 27 g (9 g saturated)
Cholesterol: 193 mg
Potassium: 695 mg
Calcium: 100 mg
Sodium: 188 mg
Iron: 15 mg

Heavenly Spiced Ribs *p. 164*
Calories: 694 kcal
Carbs: 13 g (9 g sugar, 1 g of fiber)
Protein: 66 g
Fat: 40 g (16 g saturated)
Cholesterol: 201 mg
Potassium: 1261 mg
Calcium: 35 mg
Sodium: 1003 mg
Iron: 8 mg

Maple Mustard London Broil *p. 154*
Calories: 352 kcal
Carbs: 7g (6 g sugar, 0 g of fiber)
Protein: 55 g
Fat: 9 g (3 g saturated)
Cholesterol: 136 mg
Potassium: 534 mg
Calcium: 28 mg
Sodium: 310 mg
Iron: 6 mg

Massive Meatballs, Italian Style *p. 174*
Calories: 160 kcal
Carbs: 10 g (6 g sugar, 2 g of fiber)
Protein: 16 g
Fat: 7 g (2 g saturated)
Cholesterol: 40 mg
Potassium: 72 mg
Calcium: 33 mg
Sodium: 297 mg
Iron: 3 mg

Portobello London Broil *p. 156*
Calories: 426 kcal
Carbs: 11 g (8 g sugar, 1 g of fiber)
Protein: 57 g
Fat: 16 g (4 g saturated)
Cholesterol: 136 mg
Potassium: 792 mg
Calcium: 13 mg
Sodium: 587 mg
Iron: 5 mg

Saucy Veal Spare Ribs *p. 170*
Calories: 910 kcal
Carbs: 39 g (27 g sugar, 3 g of fiber)
Protein: 91 g
Fat: 32 g (8 g saturated)
Cholesterol: 391 mg
Potassium: 1538 mg
Calcium: 81 mg
Sodium: 968 mg
Iron: 5 mg

Spiced Beef With Roasted Butternut Squash *p. 176*
Calories: 267 kcal
Carbs: 23g (5 g sugar, 4 g of fiber)
Protein: 19 g
Fat: 13 g (3 g saturated)
Cholesterol: 44 mg
Potassium: 618 mg
Calcium: 93 mg
Sodium: 59 mg
Iron: 3 mg

Stuffed Beef Cannelloni *p. 172*
Calories: 357 kcal
Carbs: 25 g (12 g sugar, 4 g of fiber)
Protein: 31 g
Fat: 15 g (4 g saturated)
Cholesterol: 71 mg
Potassium: 229 mg
Calcium: 148 mg
Sodium: 896 mg
Iron: 5 mg

Dairy

Cheese Blintz Souffle *p. 186*
Calories: 477 kcal
Carbs: 45 g (10 g sugar, 1 g of fiber)
Protein: 27 g
Fat: 22 g (13 g saturated)
Cholesterol: 176 mg
Potassium: 328 mg
Calcium: 368 mg
Sodium: 303 mg
Iron: 2 mg

Cheesy Orzo Mac & Cheese *p. 192*
Calories: 324 kcal
Carbs: 45 g (4 g sugar, 2 g of fiber)
Protein: 19 g
Fat: 7 g (4 g saturated)
Cholesterol: 20 mg
Potassium: 98 mg
Calcium: 282 mg
Sodium: 608 mg
Iron: 2 mg

Crispy Garlicky Parmesan Potatoes *p. 188*
Calories: 246 kcal
Carbs: 38 g (2 g sugar, 5 g of fiber)
Protein: 6 g
Fat: 9 g (2 g saturated)
Cholesterol: 6 mg
Potassium: 929 mg
Calcium: 106 mg
Sodium: 435 mg
Iron: 2 mg

Harvest Squash & Feta *p. 200*
Calories: 419 kcal
Carbs: 34 g (11 g sugar, 6 g of fiber)
Protein: 11 g
Fat: 27 g (5 g saturated)
Cholesterol: 13 mg
Potassium: 813 mg
Calcium: 202 mg
Sodium: 462 mg
Iron: 2 mg

Italian-Style Quinoa *p. 180*
Calories: 255 kcal
Carbs: 28 g (4 g sugar, 3 g of fiber)
Protein: 8 g
Fat: 12 g (2 g saturated)
Cholesterol: 5 mg
Potassium: 101 mg
Calcium: 58 mg
Sodium: 180 mg
Iron: 2 mg

Leek & Goat Cheese Frittata *p. 202*

Calories: 211 kcal
Carbs: 9 g (2 g sugar, 1 g of fiber)
Protein: 14 g
Fat: 15 g (7 g saturated)
Cholesterol: 324 mg
Potassium: 85 mg
Calcium: 86 mg
Sodium: 313 mg
Iron: 2 mg

Lemon Butter Asparagus *p. 196*

Calories: 132 kcal
Carbs: 5 g (2 g sugar, 3 g of fiber)
Protein: 3 g
Fat: 12 g (6 g saturated)
Cholesterol: 23 mg
Potassium: 264 mg
Calcium: 38 mg
Sodium: 80 mg
Iron: 3 mg

Potato-Crusted Quiche *p. 190*

Calories: 232 kcal
Carbs: 27 g (3 g sugar, 3 g of fiber)
Protein: 13 g
Fat: 9 G (3 g saturated)
Cholesterol: 85 mg
Potassium: 730 mg
Calcium: 209 mg
Sodium: 960 mg
Iron: 2 mg

Quinoa Granola Parfaits *p. 198*

Calories: 599 kcal
Carbs: 86 g (44 g sugar, 10 g of fiber)
Protein: 28 g
Fat: 19 g (2 g saturated)
Cholesterol: 8 mg
Potassium: 532 mg
Calcium: 269 mg
Sodium: 71 mg
Iron: 2 mg

Quinoa Pizza Ramekins *p. 182*

Calories: 177 kcal
Carbs: 23 g (5 g sugar, 3 g of fiber)
Protein: 9 g
Fat: 6 g (3 g saturated)
Cholesterol: 16 mg
Potassium: 84 mg
Calcium: 198 mg
Sodium: 241 mg
Iron: 2 mg

Spaghetti Squash Lasagna *p. 204*

Calories: 236 kcal
Carbs: 20 g (9 g sugar, 4 g of fiber)
Protein: 19 g
Fat: 10 g (6 g saturated)
Cholesterol: 32 mg
Potassium: 269 mg
Calcium: 489 mg
Sodium: 725 mg
Iron: 3 mg

Spinach, Mango & Mozzarella Salad *p. 194*

Calories: 322 kcal
Carbs: 30 g (24 g sugar, 3 g of fiber)
Protein: 11 g
Fat: 20 g (6 g saturated)
Cholesterol: 25 mg
Potassium: 217 mg
Calcium: 325 mg
Sodium: 308 mg
Iron: 2 mg

Spinach Cheese Bites *p. 184*

Calories: 73 kcal
Carbs: 5 g (0 g sugar, 1 g of fiber)
Protein: 3 g
Fat: 5 g (3 g saturated)
Cholesterol: 38 mg
Potassium: 65 mg
Calcium: 63 mg
Sodium: 177 mg
Iron: 0 mg

Grain Side Dishes

Caramelized Onion & Garlic Lentils *p. 234*

Calories: 193 kcal
Carbs: 30g (4 g sugar, 5 g of fiber)
Protein: 9 g
Fat: 5 g (1 g saturated)
Cholesterol: 0 mg
Potassium: 378 mg
Calcium: 50 mg
Sodium: 14 mg
Iron: 3 mg

Dilled Rice With Edamame & Dried Cranberries *p. 216*

Calories: 353 kcal
Carbs: 67 g (21 g sugar, 4 g of fiber)
Protein: 7 g
Fat: 6 g (1 g saturated)
Cholesterol: 0 mg
Potassium: 71 mg
Calcium: 29 mg
Sodium: 652 mg
Iron: 1 mg

Farro Tabbouli With Cherry Tomatoes *p. 232*

Calories: 228 kcal
Carbs: 29 g (4 g sugar, 4 g of fiber)
Protein: 6 g
Fat: 12 g (1 g saturated)
Cholesterol: 0 mg
Potassium: 349 mg
Calcium: 67 mg
Sodium: 112 mg
Iron: 2 mg

Israeli Couscous Salad With Asparagus & Olives *p. 208*

Calories: 372 kcal
Carbs: 50 g (9 g sugar, 5 g of fiber)
Protein: 9 g
Fat: 17 g (2 g saturated)
Cholesterol: 0 mg
Potassium: 206 mg
Calcium: 93 mg
Sodium: 530 mg
Iron: 8 mg

Mango Wild Rice *p. 214*

Calories: 296 kcal
Carbs: 58 g (31 g sugar, 4 g of fiber)
Protein: 3 g
Fat: 6 g (1 g saturated)
Cholesterol: 0 mg
Potassium: 61 mg
Calcium: 48 mg
Sodium: 261 mg
Iron: 1 mg

Mushroom & Onion Farfel *p. 228*

Calories: 339 kcal
Carbs: 51 g (5 g sugar, 4 g of fiber)
Protein: 9 g
Fat: 12 g (2 g saturated)
Cholesterol: 0 mg
Potassium: 320 mg
Calcium: 42 mg
Sodium: 498 mg
Iron: 3 mg

One-Pot Mushrooms & Rice *p. 212*
Calories: 253 kcal
Carbs: 49 g (6 g sugar, 1 g of fiber)
Protein: 6 g
Fat: 4 g (1 g saturated)
Cholesterol: 0 mg
Potassium: 198 mg
Calcium: 20 mg
Sodium: 536 mg
Iron: 0 mg

Pomegranate Almond Couscous *p. 210*
Calories: 457 kcal
Carbs: 55 g (10 g sugar, 9 g of fiber)
Protein: 15 g
Fat: 21 g (2 g saturated)
Cholesterol: 0 mg
Potassium: 272 mg
Calcium: 120 mg
Sodium: 348 mg
Iron: 2 mg

Quinoa & Sweet Potatoes *p. 220*
Calories: 319 kcal
Carbs: 48 g (21 g sugar, 5 g of fiber)
Protein: 5 g
Fat: 12 g (2 g saturated)
Cholesterol: 0 mg
Potassium: 82 mg
Calcium: 40 mg
Sodium: 326 mg
Iron: 2 mg

Rosy Quinoa *p. 222*
Calories: 358 kcal
Carbs: 54 g (15 g sugar, 7 g of fiber)
Protein: 9 g
Fat: 14 g (2 g saturated)
Cholesterol: 0 mg
Potassium: 255 mg
Calcium: 133 mg
Sodium: 476 mg
Iron: 13 mg

Terra Chip Rice Salad *p. 218*
Calories: 385 kcal
Carbs: 53 g (4 g sugar, 4 g of fiber)
Protein: 7 g
Fat: 16 g (2 g saturated)
Cholesterol: 0 mg
Potassium: 148 mg
Calcium: 30 mg
Sodium: 378 mg
Iron: 1 mg

Vegetable Barley Salad *p. 230*
Calories: 237 kcal
Carbs: 34 g (3 g sugar, 8 g of fiber)
Protein: 5 g
Fat: 10 g (1 g saturated)
Cholesterol: 0 mg
Potassium: 387 mg
Calcium: 58 mg
Sodium: 125 mg
Iron: 1 mg

Veggie Kasha & Bows *p. 226*
Calories: 149 kcal
Carbs: 21 g (5 g sugar, 3 g of fiber)
Protein: 5 g
Fat: 6 g (1 g saturated)
Cholesterol: 38 mg
Potassium: 312 mg
Calcium: 30 mg
Sodium: 504 mg
Iron: 1 mg

Zoodles, Quinoa, & More *p. 224*
Calories: 350 kcal
Carbs: 51 g (24 g sugar, 5 g of fiber)
Protein: 7 g
Fat: 15 g (2 g saturated)
Cholesterol: 0 mg
Potassium: 375 mg
Calcium: 46 mg
Sodium: 757 mg
Iron: 2 mg

Vegetable Side Dishes

Balsamic Asparagus & Tomatoes *p. 238*
Calories: 127 kcal
Carbs: 20 g (16 g sugar, 4 g of fiber)
Protein: 4 g
Fat: 5 g (1 g saturated)
Cholesterol: 0 mg
Potassium: 427 mg
Calcium: 42 mg
Sodium: 6 mg
Iron: 3 mg

Candied Cauliflower With Almonds *p. 242*
Calories: 168 kcal
Carbs: 18 g (11 g sugar, 4 g of fiber)
Protein: 5 g
Fat: 10 g (1 g saturated)
Cholesterol: 0 mg
Potassium: 428 mg
Calcium: 67 mg
Sodium: 43 mg
Iron: 2 mg

Cauliflower & Chickpeas *p. 244*
Calories: 181 kcal
Carbs: 24 g (4 g sugar, 7 g of fiber)
Protein: 8 g
Fat: 6 g (1 g saturated)
Cholesterol: 0 mg
Potassium: 623 mg
Calcium: 84 mg
Sodium: 227 mg
Iron: 2 mg

Cauliflower Rainbow "Rice" *p. 264*
Calories: 247 kcal
Carbs: 31 g (13 g sugar, 8 g of fiber)
Protein: 12 g
Fat: 10 g (2 g saturated)
Cholesterol: 113 mg
Potassium: 854 mg
Calcium: 98 mg
Sodium: 923 mg
Iron: 2 mg

Classic Potato Latkes With Assorted Toppings *p. 258*
Calories: 87 kcal (per 1 latke)
Carbs: 19 g (1 g sugar, 1 g of fiber)
Protein: 3 g
Fat: 1 g (0 g saturated)
Cholesterol: 19 mg
Potassium: 415 mg
Calcium: 24 mg
Sodium: 92 mg
Iron: 1 mg

Mustard & Garlic Roasted Potatoes *p. 248*
Calories: 696 kcal
Carbs: 149 g (13 g sugar, 20 g of fiber)
Protein: 17 g
Fat: 6 g (1 g saturated)
Cholesterol: 0 mg
Potassium: 4003 mg
Calcium: 110 mg
Sodium: 637 mg
Iron: 6 mg

Oven-Baked French Fries With Tahini Drizzle *p. 246*

Calories: 559 kcal
Carbs: 64 g (3 g sugar, 8 g of fiber)
Protein: 13 g
Fat: 30 g (4 g saturated)
Cholesterol: 0 mg
Potassium: 1606 mg
Calcium: 104 mg
Sodium: 51 mg
Iron: 5 mg

Panko-Topped Squash Crescents *p. 262*

Calories: 173 kcal
Carbs: 26 g (9 g sugar, 1 g of fiber)
Protein: 2 g
Fat: 7 g (1 g saturated)
Cholesterol: 0 mg
Potassium: 234 mg
Calcium: 37 mg
Sodium: 29 mg
Iron: 1 mg

Peas & Mushrooms *p. 240*

Calories: 148 kcal
Carbs: 17 g (6 g sugar, 5 g of fiber)
Protein: 6 g
Fat: 7 g (1 g saturated)
Cholesterol: 0 mg
Potassium: 466 mg
Calcium: 32 mg
Sodium: 407 mg
Iron: 2 mg

Roasted Carrots, Parsnips & Sweet Potatoes *p. 254*

Calories: 298 kcal
Carbs: 52 g (21 g sugar, 9 g of fiber)
Protein: 4 g
Fat: 10 g (2 g saturated)
Cholesterol: 0 mg
Potassium: 977 mg
Calcium: 114 mg
Sodium: 568 mg
Iron: 2 mg

Roasted Sweet & Savory Mushrooms *p. 260*

Calories: 202 kcal
Carbs: 25 g (15 g sugar, 3 g of fiber)
Protein: 5 g
Fat: 11 g (2 g saturated)
Cholesterol: 0 mg
Potassium: 709 mg
Calcium: 17 mg
Sodium: 444 mg
Iron: 1 mg

Roasted Vegetables With Terra Chips *p. 252*

Calories: 233 kcal
Carbs: 39 g (18 g sugar, 5 g of fiber)
Protein: 3 g
Fat: 9 g (1 g saturated)
Cholesterol: 0 mg
Potassium: 587 mg
Calcium: 69 mg
Sodium: 73 mg
Iron: 2 mg

Sesame Sweet Potatoes *p. 250*

Calories: 252 kcal
Carbs: 38 g (15 g sugar, 5 g of fiber)
Protein: 4 g
Fat: 10 g (1 g saturated)
Cholesterol: 0 mg
Potassium: 487 mg
Calcium: 78 mg
Sodium: 566 mg
Iron: 1 mg

Sweet Potato Gratin With Maple Granola Topping *p. 256*

Calories: 310 kcal
Carbs: 38 g (14 g sugar, 5 g of fiber)
Protein: 6 g
Fat: 16 g (2 g saturated)
Cholesterol: 0 mg
Potassium: 279 mg
Calcium: 59 mg
Sodium: 59 mg
Iron: 2 mg

Cookies & Treats

Brown Sugar Peach Crisp *p. 292*

Calories: 310 kcal
Carbs: 54 g (33 g sugar, 4 g of fiber)
Protein: 4 g
Fat: 11 g (2 g saturated)
Cholesterol: 0 mg
Potassium: 314 mg
Calcium: 16 mg
Sodium: 0 mg
Iron: 2 mg

Chocolate Bark *p. 276*

Seedy Chocolate Bark

Calories: 403 kcal
Carbs: 49 g (28 g sugar, 11 g of fiber)
Protein: 11 g
Fat: 23 g (9 g saturated)
Cholesterol: 0 mg
Potassium: 0 mg
Calcium: 92 mg
Sodium: 46 mg
Iron: 4 mg

White Chocolate Bark

Calories: 527 kcal
Carbs: 61 g (52 g sugar, 5 g of fiber)
Protein: 9 g
Fat: 28 g (11 g saturated)
Cholesterol: 11 mg
Potassium: 278 mg
Calcium: 100 mg
Sodium: 105 mg
Iron: 1 mg

Cookie Chocolate Bark

Calories: 297 kcal
Carbs: 39 g (28 g sugar, 3 g of fiber)
Protein: 3 g
Fat: 17 g (9 g saturated)
Cholesterol: 1 mg
Potassium: 0 mg
Calcium: 0 mg
Sodium: 33 mg
Iron: 0 mg

Nutella Chocolate Bark

Calories: 663 kcal
Carbs: 61 g (50 g sugar, 7 g of fiber)
Protein: 11 g
Fat: 46 g (16 g saturated)
Cholesterol: 0 mg
Potassium: 0 mg
Calcium: 65 mg
Sodium: 159 mg
Iron: 3 mg

Chocolate Chip Granola Cookies *p. 272*

Calories: 203 kcal
Carbs: 30 g (18 g sugar, 2 g of fiber)
Protein: 3 g
Fat: 9 g (3 g saturated)
Cholesterol: 19 mg
Potassium: 46 mg
Calcium: 23 mg
Sodium: 77 mg
Iron: 1 mg

Chocolate Chip Popcorn Blondies *p. 278*
Calories: 188 kcal
Carbs: 24 g (7 g sugar, 2 g of fiber)
Protein: 3 g
Fat: 11 g (5 g saturated)
Cholesterol: 13 mg
Potassium: 12 mg
Calcium: 1 mg
Sodium: 40 mg
Iron: 1 mg

Chocolate Coconut Biscotti *p. 274*
Calories: 84 kcal
Carbs: 13 g (4 g sugar, 1 g of fiber)
Protein: 2 g
Fat: 4 g (3 g saturated)
Cholesterol: 14 mg
Potassium: 7 mg
Calcium: 1 mg
Sodium: 32 mg
Iron: 1 mg

Chocolate Dipped Pineapple *p. 290*
Calories: 507 kcal
Carbs: 77 g (67 g sugar, 7 g of fiber)
Protein: 7 g
Fat: 22 g (11 g saturated)
Cholesterol: 0 mg
Potassium: 367 mg
Calcium: 19 mg
Sodium: 16 mg
Iron: 2 mg

Chocolate Mounds *p. 268*
Calories: 130 kcal
Carbs: 19 g (12 g sugar, 2 g of fiber)
Protein: 2 g
Fat: 6 g (3 g saturated)
Cholesterol: 0 mg
Potassium: 9 mg
Calcium: 2 mg
Sodium: 86 mg
Iron: 1 mg

Chocolate Peanut Butter Bites *p. 282*
Calories: 574 kcal
Carbs: 104 g (31 g sugar, 11 g of fiber)
Protein: 12 g
Fat: 18 g (9 g saturated)
Cholesterol: 0 mg
Potassium: 232 mg
Calcium: 144 mg
Sodium: 458 mg
Iron: 21 mg

Crispy Peanut Butter Bars *p. 286*
Calories: 161 kcal
Carbs: 24 g (10 g sugar, 2 g of fiber)
Protein: 4 g
Fat: 7 g (3 g saturated)
Cholesterol: 0 mg
Potassium: 20 mg
Calcium: 8 mg
Sodium: 98 mg
Iron: 2 mg

No-Bake Energy Bites *p. 288*
Calories: 199 kcal
Carbs: 25 g (16 g sugar, 4 g of fiber)
Protein: 5 g
Fat: 9 g (2 g saturated)
Cholesterol: 0 mg
Potassium: 63 mg
Calcium: 22 mg
Sodium: 27 mg
Iron: 1 mg

Orange-Infused Chocolate Chip Muffins *p. 284*
Calories: 337 kcal
Carbs: 37 g (12 g sugar, 2 g of fiber)
Protein: 4 g
Fat: 22 g (7 g saturated)
Cholesterol: 38 mg
Potassium: 88 mg
Calcium: 18 mg
Sodium: 121 mg
Iron: 2 mg

Peanut Butter Cookie Brownies *p. 280*
Calories: 166 kcal
Carbs: 26 g (19 g sugar, 2 g of fiber)
Protein: 5 g
Fat: 7 g (1 g saturated)
Cholesterol: 53 mg
Potassium: 9 mg
Calcium: 18 mg
Sodium: 60 mg
Iron: 1 mg

The Ultimate Chewy Chocolate Brownie Cookie *p. 270*
Calories: 279 kcal
Carbs: 39 g (24 g sugar, 3 g of fiber)
Protein: 3 g
Fat: 15 g (5 g saturated)
Cholesterol: 30 mg
Potassium: 11 mg
Calcium: 3 mg
Sodium: 53 mg
Iron: 1 mg

Cakes

Apple Crumble Pie *p. 304*
Calories: 532 kcal
Carbs: 73 g (35 g sugar, 3 g of fiber)
Protein: 5 g
Fat: 28 g (4 g saturated)
Cholesterol: 0 mg
Potassium: 231 mg
Calcium: 17 mg
Sodium: 241 mg
Iron: 2 mg

Blueberry Lemon Cake *p. 298*
Calories: 355 kcal
Carbs: 43 g (21 g sugar, 2 g of fiber)
Protein: 5 g
Fat: 20 g (3 g saturated)
Cholesterol: 75 mg
Potassium: 206 mg
Calcium: 68 mg
Sodium: 190 mg
Iron: 1 mg

Chocolate Zucchini Cake *p. 308*
Calories: 430 kcal
Carbs: 56 g (35 g sugar, 3 g of fiber)
Protein: 7 g
Fat: 23 g (4 g saturated)
Cholesterol: 56 mg
Potassium: 232 mg
Calcium: 68 mg
Sodium: 182 mg
Iron: 2 mg

Classic Pecan Pie *p. 306*
Calories: 464 kcal
Carbs: 53 g (39 g sugar, 2 g of fiber)
Protein: 5 g
Fat: 29 g (4 g saturated)
Cholesterol: 68 mg
Potassium: 86 mg
Calcium: 21 mg
Sodium: 47 mg
Iron: 1 mg

Cranberry Chocolate Chip Cake *p. 296*
Calories: 355 kcal
Carbs: 39 g (23 g sugar, 2 g of fiber)
Protein: 4 g
Fat: 23 g (6 g saturated)
Cholesterol: 42 mg
Potassium: 173 mg
Calcium: 24 mg
Sodium: 167 mg
Iron: 1 mg

Crumb-Topped Pumpkin Cake *p. 310*

Calories: 444 kcal
Carbs: 59 g (30 g sugar, 5 g of fiber)
Protein: 8 g
Fat: 23 g (9 g saturated)
Cholesterol: 13 mg
Potassium: 126 mg
Calcium: 145 mg
Sodium: 97 mg
Iron: 2 mg

Granola Ice Cream Cake *p. 312*

Calories: 444 kcal
Carbs: 59 g (30 g sugar, 5 g of fiber)
Protein: 8 g
Fat: 23 g (9 g saturated)
Cholesterol: 13 mg
Potassium: 126 mg
Calcium: 145 mg
Sodium: 97 mg
Iron: 2 mg

Key Lime Pie *p. 314*

Calories: 461 kcal
Carbs: 82 g (70 g sugar, 1 g of fiber)
Protein: 10 g
Fat: 10 g (5 g saturated)
Cholesterol: 34 mg
Potassium: 63 mg
Calcium: 296 mg
Sodium: 202 mg
Iron: 1 mg

Light & Fluffy Chiffon Cake *p. 300*

Calories: 206 kcal
Carbs: 25 g (15 g sugar, 0 g of fiber)
Protein: 6 g
Fat: 12 g (2 g saturated)
Cholesterol: 180 mg
Potassium: 15 mg
Calcium: 16 mg
Sodium: 68 mg
Iron: 1 mg

Raspberry Swirl White Chocolate Cheesecake *p. 316*

Calories: 503 kcal
Carbs: 77 g (60 g sugar, 1 g of fiber)
Protein: 18 g
Fat: 18 g (10 g saturated)
Cholesterol: 104 mg
Potassium: 338 mg
Calcium: 365 mg
Sodium: 696 mg
Iron: 1 mg

Salted Chocolate Ganache Tart *p. 302*

Calories: 452 kcal
Carbs: 38 g (21 g sugar, 3 g of fiber)
Protein: 4 g
Fat: 34 g (14 g saturated)
Cholesterol: 72 mg
Potassium: 21 mg
Calcium: 2 mg
Sodium: 7 mg
Iron: 1 mg

Index

NOTE: Page references in *bold italic* refer to recipe variations or tips found under Norene's Notes.

Thank You

To all my recipe testers — you've played a crucial role in getting these dishes ready for the big debut. Thank you for your time, dedication, and thoughtful insights, and I hope you had some fun in the kitchen, too!

Laila Alter, Rosalie Antman, Cindy Beer, Tali Berger, Saralee Bernstein, Tania Black, Miriam Burke, Rita Bleicher, Chavi Breitbart, Brenda Borzykowski, Victoria Carreiro, Sarah Casden, Rhonda Charlat, Yael Diamond, Hilary Edelstein, Robyn Feldberg, Elizabeth Fishel, Marcie Fisher, Aliza Fried, Marilyn Glick, Naomi Glustein, Ann Goldman, Ariella Goldstein, Simone Greenbaum, Daniella Greenspan, Esther Gurman, Rivka Hamburger, Aimee Hass, Betty Hainsfurther, Hedy Halpern, Natalie Hirschel, Sheri Horlick, Shoshana Israel, Deborah Jacobs, Eileen Jadd, Marsha Johnston, Sonya Kaplan, Chani Kaplan, Yael Katzman, Orah Katzman, Lisa Kasner Schacter, Sharonne Katz, Sharon Kravetsky, Carol Kosters, Jennifer Knight, Shoshana Lankelevic, Sara Lass, Norene Lax, Hadassah Lebovic, Neal and Robyn Lerner, Rachel Libman, Cheryl Liederman, Resa Litwack, Miri Lazarescu, Marla Marcus, Karen Meyer, Rena Neufeld, Devora Paskowitz, Carol Rabinovitch, Hailey Remer, Emma Rinberg, Suzy Rose, P'nina Rosenberg, MaryAnn Rosenbloom, Sharon Schach, Shoshana Schachter, Sherri Segal, Talya Silver, Bonny Silver, Ilana Segal, Tova Segal, Esther Shields, Shelley Shields, Shayna Swartz, Talia Shainhouse, Deena Shlagbaum, Nicole Shuckett, Miryam Smilow, Josh Steinberg, Kira Sunshine, Judy Szamosi, Chantal Ulmer, Ariella Vatenmakher, Racheli Veres, Ali Veres, Noa Voss, Linda Warner, Dova Weinberger, Dori Weiss, Alyssa Wiesel, Carla Wertman, Joelle Yavin, Dalia Yunger